D0997113

Chocolate Classics

BARBARA GRUNES AND PHYLLIS MAGIDA

CONTEMPORARY
BOOKS

CHICAGO

Library of Congress Cataloging-in-Publication Data

Grunes, Barbara.
Chocolate classics / Barbara Grunes and Phyllis Magida.
p. cm.
Includes bibliographical references and index.
ISBN 0-8092-3700-8 (cloth)
1. Cookery (Chocolate) 2. Desserts.
3. Chocolate. I. Magida, Phyllis. II. Title.
TX767.C5G75 1993
641.6'374—dc20 93-27084
CIP

Published by Contemporary Books, Inc.
Two Prudential Plaza, Chicago, Illinois 60601-6790
Manufactured in the United States of America
International Standard Book Number: 0-8092-3700-8
10 9 8 7 6 5 4 3 2 1

Contents

Introduction

No doubt about it, we're crazy about chocolate. But so are millions of other people all over the world. And no one would argue that writing a chocolate book is just plain *fun.*

But those aren't the only reasons we wanted to write this book. Truth is, we had a number of chocolate recipes inside of us just waiting to get out.

These include forties classics, like Brownstone Front Cake, also known as a cake in a glass dish, and fifties classics, such as our Great American Chocolate Cake. They also include recent classics such as our Dutch Flourless Chocolate Cake, which was so popular in the eighties, and even a nineties classic—the intensely chocolate Queen of Sheba Cake. We serve it surrounded by a crème anglaise that is dotted with brilliantly colored fruits and almonds, reminiscent of the jewels Sheba gave to King Solomon.

Some of our cakes are chocolate versions of southern classics—like our Chocolate Baltimore and our Chocolate Kentucky Bourbon Pecan cakes. Others are European classics, such as our Viennese Sacher Torte and our English Steamed Chocolate Pudding. Still others are classic family heirlooms, such as Aunt Ida's Marble Cake—a thirties favorite.

We also include instructions for giving a chocolate tea according to Fiona Merriweather, an English friend now living in this country.

Although our recipes are classic, our techniques are contemporary. Instead of folding beaten egg whites into cake batters, for example, we update the procedure by

adding some of the sugar in the recipe to the whites; the resultant meringue is stiffer and folds more easily into a batter. And instead of adding ordinary vinegar to milk to sour it, we suggest using fruit or spice vinegars, like raspberry or nutmeg for chocolate cakes, because they impart an extra, albeit subtle, flavor to the batter.

On the other hand, we do not say "butter or margarine." If you're going to go to the time and expense of making an elegant chocolate dish, don't diminish its taste by using margarine. If necessary, simply save these recipes for special occasions.

We thoroughly enjoyed writing this book, part of it done during American Chocolate Week, March 14-20. And we must confess that between us we gained a total of 16 pounds. We hope you enjoy making and eating these classics as much as we did baking and eating them.

Barbara Grunes and Phyllis Magida
Chicago

Montezuma's Favorite Drink

Botanists agree that the first cocoa trees—*Theobroma cacao*—grew wild about 4,000 years ago, either in the Amazon Basin in Brazil, the Orinoco Valley of Venezuela, or somewhere in Central America. But no one has any idea when the first canny Indian thought to ferment, dry, roast, and hull a cacao (or cocoa) bean, grind it up into a powder, then mix this powder with liquid and drink it. But whoever first served it to the village, this thick, cold, frothy, bitter chocolate drink became so popular that the Indians took the cocoa bean with them on their trading expeditions. It probably arrived in the Yucatán around A.D. 600.

The Mayans thought so highly of chocolate that they ultimately used it as currency: 4 beans would buy a squash, 10 a rabbit or a night with a prostitute, and 100 a slave.

The Aztecs also cultivated chocolate, and soon a whole legend had grown up around it: a fair-skinned bearded god named Quetzalcoatl had come down from the Land of Gold to rule the Aztecs, bringing with him knowledge of painting, maize, metal craft, and a few cocoa beans. According to the legend, Quetzalcoatl ruled wisely for many years. But another god tricked him into drinking a magic potion that took away his powers. Sadly, he buried his wealth and returned to the Land of Gold. Before he left, he promised his people one thing: to return every 52 years in the year of "One Reed" on the Aztec calendar.

Coincidentally, when the fair-skinned, bearded Hernán Cortés arrived at the Aztec capital Tenochtitlán in 1519, it was the year of "One Reed." The Aztec ruler Montezuma II welcomed Cortés royally, thinking he was Quetzalcoatl. The welcoming drink served was, of course, a cup of thick, frothy, cold unsweetened chocolate.

Cortés didn't take to chocolate instantly; unsweetened chocolate is, after all, an acquired taste. But he knew currency when he saw it. Not only did he send the plant to Spain; he also planted Spanish "money" plantations—that is, cacao—wherever he could. Since the plant grows only in a narrow band around the center of the Earth, approximately 20 degrees north to 20 degrees south of the equator, he planted cacao beans in Central and South America, in the Caribbean, and in the Philippines.

The Dutch, who came in on the industry in the late 17th century, helped spread the word and the bean to Indonesia, Sri Lanka (then Ceylon), and the West African islands of Sao Tomé and Bioko (formerly Fernando Po). From there the tree spread to Africa's west coast, forming the basis for today's gigantic modern chocolate industries. Africa's Ivory Coast and Brazil are today the leading producers of cacao beans, followed by Ghana, Nigeria, and several other countries.

Actually, Christopher Columbus had come across chocolate beans perhaps as much as 17 years earlier when he landed in Nicaragua. But when he brought them home to King Ferdinand, no one paid much attention to them.

It wasn't until Cortés returned to Spain in 1528, bringing with him three chests of cocoa beans, growing

and processing techniques, and a recipe for Montezuma's favorite drink, that chocolate received its due.

All chocolate production was immediately taken over by the best cooks in town—the monks in their cloisters. The monks experimented and perfected the roasting, grinding, and shaping processes. They ended up with tablets of chocolate paste, which could then be dissolved in cups of liquid.

It was in Spain that the cold, bitter chocolate drink evolved into a hot, sugared beverage, sometimes seasoned with vanilla, rose or orange flower water or spiced with cinnamon, nutmeg, or allspice.

The Spanish managed to keep chocolate, its production, and the art of the industry a secret for almost a century. In fact, when Dutch and English pirates found cocoa beans in the holds of Spanish ships, they had no idea what they were and threw them overboard.

But the secret got out of the bag when Antonio Carletti, an Italian visitor to Spain, took the chocolate drink recipe home to Italy in 1606. The Italians were crazy about chocolate. But in 1662 its consumption was qualified by fears that the drink was too worldly and sensual to enjoy during Lent. Cardinal Brancaccio of Rome pondered the problem and relieved everyone's fears: "*Liquidum non frangit jejunum,*" he said. "Liquids"—he meant chocolate of course—"do not break the fast."

France was introduced to chocolate by the Jews, who brought it with them from Spain and settled near Bayonne. Chocolate appreciation was limited to Bayonne, however, until 1615, when Anne of Austria, then 14, took a box of chocolates to France for her 14-year-old fiancé, Louis XIII. The French court was immediately crazy about chocolate, and members of the French Court vied for invitations to "the chocolate of her Royal Highness."

Then, in 1657, a French businessman took the boat to England and opened the first English chocolate house. The English were no less crazy for chocolate, and dozens of fashionable chocolate houses quickly opened all over London. Soon the chocolate-drinking habit had spread all over Europe.

Chocolate recrossed the ocean during this time, and Americans became as crazy about a cup of chocolate as the Europeans were. Then, in about 1750, we went into the business when Massachusetts sea captains brought home cocoa beans from the Caribbean, which they sold to American shopkeepers. In turn, these shopkeepers processed the beans and sold them to a waiting public.

The first American chocolate factory—Hannon Chocolate Company—opened in 1765 when a chocolate maker from Ireland, John Hannon, formed a partnership with a physician from Massachusetts, Dr. James Baker. The company became the Baker Company in 1779, when, alas, Hannon sailed off to buy cocoa beans and was lost somewhere in the West Indies.

Until 1765 chocolate had been ground by hand—either with a mortar and pestle, as in the Yucatán, or between stone disks. But James Watt's invention of the steam engine changed the texture of chocolate forever.

The Hannon Chocolate Company was located on the banks of Massachusetts's Neponset River; soon the Hannon and Baker Company was using water power to grind the cocoa beans, which gave the finished chocolate a silkier texture than was possible with hand grinding.

But everyone was still only *drinking* chocolate. It wasn't until 1828, when Dutch chemist Coenraad van

Houten invented a "chocolate press," that an *eating* chocolate recipe was made possible. Van Houten's press separated the beans into cocoa butter and a powdery chocolate liquor. Van Houten marketed the powdery stuff to make the hot chocolate everyone was drinking. But he wasn't sure what to do with the cocoa butter.

Nineteen years later, in 1847, an English chocolate company—Fry & Sons—came up with the idea that solid chocolate might catch on. With the now extracted cocoa butter as an ingredient to work with, they experimented a little and created a good recipe using cocoa butter, chocolate liquor, and sugar. Soon the first "eating" chocolate was on the market.

In the next 30 years solid chocolate continued to evolve. First milk chocolate was created when two canny Swiss businessmen, Daniel Peter and Henri Nestlé, added condensed milk to chocolate liquor and sugar. Then, in 1880, another Swiss businessman, Rodolphe Lindt, invented a process known today as *conching* (see "A Few Chocolate Terms"), which took the English eating-chocolate idea to Swiss melt-in-your-mouth heights.

Today there are numerous chocolate companies on every continent—except Antarctica of course—throughout the world.

A FEW CHOCOLATE TERMS

Chocolate: a flavoring, beverage, candy or coating that is prepared from grinding the cocoa nibs—small pieces of roasted cacao beans.

Chocolate liquor: the thick dark brown paste, often called chocolate *matter,* that results when the nibs are crushed under pressure, which causes some cocoa butter to melt off. The word *liquor* means a liquid, not an alcoholic liquid.

Cocoa butter: the vegetable fat derived from the nibs in the cacao bean. It is pale in color and has a low—89-93°F—melting point

Conching: a flavor and texture development process invented by Rodolphe Lindt in 1880. Chocolate liquor and apportioned amounts of cocoa butter are put in vats and heated to 130-180°F. Giant rollers then slowly agitate and aerate the chocolate for from a few hours to several days. As the chocolate particles increase in smoothness, a soft film of cocoa butter forms around each one. The temperature of the vats and hours of agitation determine the different tastes and textures of the chocolate.

Types of Chocolate

BITTER OR BAKING CHOCOLATE

Also called *unsweetened* chocolate, this is hardened chocolate liquor containing no sugar, though it may contain flavorings such as vanilla. The FDA standards of identity dictate that any chocolate labeled *bitter* or *baking* must contain at least 50 percent but no more than 58 percent cocoa butter. Since the nibs contain about 53 percent cocoa butter and 47 percent chocolate matter before they're even processed, the manufacturer has to add the cocoa butter to the chocolate liquor after they've been separated.

COCOA

Cocoa is the powder that results after chocolate liquor is put in a chocolate press, separated from some of its cocoa butter, then hardened into cakes that are pulverized and sifted.

DUTCH COCOA

This type of cocoa has been processed with an alkali, which reduces the acid in the cocoa, giving it a darker appearance and a mellower flavor. *Dutch cocoa can be used interchangeably with regular cocoa in any recipe in this book calling for cocoa.*

MILK CHOCOLATE

This is chocolate liquor to which cocoa butter, milk, sweeteners, and flavorings are added. FDA standards fix the chocolate liquor minimum at 10 percent and whole milk minimum at 12 percent. It contains about 27 percent fat. This chocolate is both eaten and used in baking.

PREMELTED CHOCOLATE

This combination of powdered cocoa and hydrogenated vegetable oil is not designated as chocolate by the FDA. We do not recommend using it.

SEMISWEET OR BITTERSWEET CHOCOLATE

Sweeteners and additional cocoa butter are added to chocolate liquor to make this type of chocolate. The FDA, which uses the terms *semisweet* and *bittersweet* interchangeably, insists that chocolates with these labels contain at least 35 percent chocolate liquor, but some professionals insist it should be more like 50 percent. The Chocolate Manufacturers Association in McLean, Virginia, adds that the fat content of either of these chocolates "averages 27 percent."

There are dozens of brands of chocolate labeled *semisweet* and *bittersweet.* We've found that those labeled *bittersweet* seem to be slightly less sweet than those labeled *semisweet when both are made by the same company.* However, we've also found that one company's bittersweet may be sweeter than another company's semisweet. In baking, then, we use the following rule: use any good-quality brand of either semisweet or bittersweet when the recipe calls for either one. This chocolate is both eaten and used in baking.

SWEET CHOCOLATE

To make sweet chocolate, extra sweeteners (more than for semisweet or bittersweet) are added to the chocolate liquor. FDA standards require sweet chocolate to contain at least 15 percent chocolate liquor. It contains about 27 percent fat. This chocolate is both eaten and used in baking. It is sometimes called *dark sweet chocolate*.

WHITE CHOCOLATE

The FDA says the term *white chocolate* is a misnomer since real chocolate must contain chocolate liquor and white chocolate does not. White chocolate gets that name from the inclusion of cocoa butter, which gives it a faint, delicate chocolate flavor. White chocolate also contains sugar, milk solids, and flavorings. Since manufacturers can't use the term *white chocolate*, they market it under a number of different names: cocoa butter coating, *chocolat blanc*, ivory and white couverture, to name a few. The amount of cocoa butter in brands of white chocolate varies greatly, from as much as 55 percent to as little as 25 percent. White chocolate is both eaten and used in baking.

CHOCOLATE BITS, MORSELS, OR CHIPS

These teardrop-shaped pieces of chocolate measure about $\frac{2}{5}$ inch across and $\frac{2}{5}$ inch high. They will soften during baking but not lose their shape, because they contain ingredients that increase their viscosity (resistance to flow). Morsels are available in milk, semisweet, minted semisweet, and white chocolate. Smaller morsels are also available.

Tips and Techniques for Working with Chocolate

STORING

Store chocolate in a dry place where the temperature stays at 68–78°F. When chocolate sits where the temperature rises above 78°F, it can "bloom," which means it appears discolored because the cocoa butter melts and rises to the surface. If this happens, the chocolate can still be used. When chocolate is stored in the refrigerator, it will sweat when brought to room temperature. Before melting, wipe it off thoroughly with paper towels; otherwise the chocolate may absorb the released liquid during melting and harden.

MELTING SWEET, UNSWEETENED, WHITE, AND SEMISWEET CHOCOLATE

Never melt chocolate over high heat or it may scorch. Place it in the top of a double boiler above gently simmering water. Take care that the top of the double boiler does not come in contact with the water. Make sure that the water does not boil furiously or the chocolate may absorb a few drops of the steam, which will cause it to stiffen into an unusable mass. For fastest results, chop chocolate into small pieces before melting, remove it when it is just barely melted, and stir until thoroughly melted.

If the recipe calls for cooling the melted chocolate before using, place the top portion of the double boiler in a cool place in your kitchen—not the refrigerator—for

a few minutes.

Don't substitute morsels when a recipe calls for unsweetened, sweet, or semisweet chocolate; morsels are formulated with a higher viscosity (resistance to flow) than blocks of chocolate and will not melt as smoothly.

Chocolate can be melted in the microwave in a microwave-safe dish if great care is taken. Microwave on HIGH for about 2 minutes. If the chocolate stays in the microwave too long, it can become rubbery. Stir until smooth after removing it from the microwave.

Take extra precautions when melting white chocolate: it is very fragile.

USING COCOA

Sift cocoa by rubbing it through a strainer onto a paper plate. Then spoon it into the measuring cup until it is overflowing slightly. Use a knife to level it. Fold the paper plate slightly to pour excess back into the cocoa tin.

A Fudge Memory

When I was 11, I was a little fat and had no waist—two facts that didn't bother me at all but bothered my parents quite a bit; enough, anyway, for them to suggest that I take ballet lessons. Perhaps they hoped that this would force a waist where none had been or at the least keep me out of harm's way, which meant out of the candy store on the corner.

The fact was, I loved fudge! Not the creamy fondant kind that is paddled on a slab until it melts down your throat. The kind I coveted was hard and slightly gritty; it kept you happy because it lasted a long time in your mouth; but it also kept you fat, because fudge has 150 calories an ounce and, when you are 11, goes right to your waist.

So, obediently, once a week I rode the subway down and the elevator up to take my ballet lesson in Chicago's Fine Arts Building at Miss Edna McRae's School of the Dance. And accordingly for one hour, I lifted legs, pointed toes, stretched, leaped, and pliéd, to finish the lesson and hurry downstairs to the fudge concession stand on the first floor.

The four-ounce piece I always bought cost 15 cents, with or without nuts. And it was always chocolate, never maple or vanilla. Also, it was wrapped cunningly (I thought) in cellophane, so you could see it shine on top if you held it under a light.

But Miss McRae hated fudge as she hated all candy, viewing it generically as an enemy of the dance. And I suspect that, if allowed, she would have taken her pointer stick to the concession stand—the same stick, incidentally, that she used not only to beat time but also to hit any one of us hard on the arch when our barre work displeased her. And I seemed to displease her a lot, judging by the bruises I accumulated weekly.

In fact I was a most unlikely candidate for the dance, at least by comparison with the big girls. I was fat, and my hair was thin. I was concave where I should have been convex.

The big girls, though, who ate all the fudge they wanted, had slim waists and elegant legs that curved backward like bananas. Also, they had thick hair.

Perhaps these facts should have encouraged me to work upward toward the dance; but in fact they catapulted me downward toward the fudge. Six days a week I ate fudge because it was chocolaty and gritty. But on Thursdays I ate it not only to compensate for the hour spent with Miss McRae and her stick but also because I was an ugly duckling forced to look at the swans.

As the term neared its end, I waited longingly for the last class, but when it came it brought fresh trouble. "Come to my office later," Miss McRae hissed in my ear, making me so nervous it ruined my barre work for the rest of the hour.

After class I reluctantly made my way to her office, worrying also that the concession stand might close if she didn't make it snappy.

"Ah," she said when she saw me, pupils glinting. "I want to talk to you." When she pointed to the small couch instead of to the chair that faced her desk, my heart sank. I knew about that couch. That was where she sat her students when she intended to have one of her famous heart-to-heart talks.

"I think," she continued when we were seated, "that I can make you into a real dancer. It will take 15 years," she continued enthusiastically. "Five to be good, 10 to be professional, and 15 to be really fine."

I stared at her without speaking, horrified at the prospect. Then suddenly, as I began crying, with all the attendant sniffles and sound effects, Miss McRae seemed to soften, thinking perhaps that she had offended the delicate sensibilities of a dancer. She had not. She had made me frantic with the idea of all those years spent there in her studio, with the stick and the dance and all those terribly beautiful girls, the fudge notwithstanding.

"Don't worry, I'm fine," I told her, searching meanwhile for something that would explain my odd behavior. Suddenly I had it.

"Miss McRae," I said emphatically, pawing around in my gym bag for a tissue. "I can't study dancing anymore. I can't ever study again. We're moving to Afghanistan in two weeks."

This was, of course, a most absurd lie. But at the time Afghanistan was the farthest place that came to mind.

"Oh," she said, giving me a long look. "That changes things. Well then, perhaps you can study there."

A few minutes later I stood happily before the concession stand on the first floor. The fudge lay there, wrapped in cellophane, as beautiful as ever. But this time, instead of buying just one four-ounce package, I bought two, before running fast, without regret, in the direction of the subway.

P.M.

Recipes

"And every time he went by . . . he would hold his nose high in the air and take long deep sniffs of the gorgeous chocolatey smell all around him."

From *Charlie and the Chocolate Factory* by
Roald Dahl

Aunt Ida's Marble Cake

MAKES 12 SERVINGS

I remember so vividly the days of my childhood in Massachusetts's Revere Beach, when my aunt Ida would make the rich, delicious marble cakes for which she was renowned. Aunt Ida's marble cakes were always (and only) made on special occasions, particularly on the Fourth of July and for family birthdays.

3 cups cake flour
2 teaspoons baking powder
¼ teaspoon salt
1 cup (2 sticks) unsalted butter at room temperature
1½ cups granulated sugar
5 large eggs
1 teaspoon vanilla extract
⅔ cup milk
½ cup unsweetened cocoa
Confectioners' sugar

1. Place a rack in the center of the oven and preheat to 375°F. Grease and flour a Bundt pan.

2. Sift the flour, baking powder, and salt together. Set aside.

3. In the large bowl of an electric mixer, cream the butter until soft, about 3 minutes. Add 1¼ cups of the granulated sugar and beat until smooth, about 3 minutes. Add the eggs, one at a time, beating well after each addition. Blend in the vanilla.

4. Add the flour mixture to the batter, alternating with enough milk (about ⅓ cup) to form a smooth dough.

5. Pour three-quarters of the batter into the prepared Bundt pan. Blend the cocoa, remaining ¼ cup sugar, and remaining ⅓ cup milk into the remaining batter. Mix until smooth.

6. With a tablespoon, drop the chocolate mixture onto the batter in the pan. Using a knife, gently swirl the chocolate through the batter to make a marbled design.

7. Bake the cake for 50–60 minutes or until a toothpick or bamboo skewer inserted in the center comes out clean. Cool the cake in the pan on a rack for 5 minutes. Invert onto a wire rack and cool completely. Transfer to a serving plate and sprinkle with sifted confectioners' sugar.

Steamed Chocolate Pudding with Butterscotch Sauce

MAKES 8 SERVINGS

Steamed pudding is a traditional dessert that is just as delicious today as it was years ago. This is actually a light and spongy cake set in a pool of butterscotch sauce that provides a pleasing taste contrast.

Steamed puddings may be cooked in a variety of glazed ceramic molds, metal pudding molds, even cleaned coffee or large juice cans. A pudding mold is a worthwhile investment if you decide to add steamed puddings to your cooking repertoire. We used a 1-quart decorative metal mold for this recipe. If the mold you use does not have a tight-fitting lid, cover the top of the mold tightly with aluminum foil. The inside of the lid should be greased liberally and then dusted with sugar. To prevent air bubbles, compact the pudding mixture and tap the mold several times.

To steam the pudding, use a large steamer, a heavy kettle, or a pot with a close-fitting lid. The vessel must be large enough to allow for good circulation of the steam around the mold.

STEAMED PUDDING

½ cup (1 stick) unsalted butter at room temperature
¾ cup granulated sugar
¾ cup all-purpose flour
3 tablespoons Dutch cocoa
¼ teaspoon baking powder

3 large eggs
3/4 teaspoon vanilla extract
1/4 cup heavy cream

BUTTERSCOTCH SAUCE
2 cups firmly packed light brown sugar
1/2 cup (1 stick) unsalted butter
1 cup heavy cream
1 1/2 teaspoons vanilla extract

1. Heavily butter a 1-quart metal steaming mold or glass dish suitable for steaming. Insert a metal trivet or rack in a steamer. Add water to just below the trivet and set the steamer on the stove to begin heating the water.

2. In the large bowl of an electric mixer, beat the butter until light, about 3 minutes. Add the sugar and continue beating for 3–4 minutes, scraping down the sides of the bowl with a rubber spatula.

3. Sift the flour, cocoa, and baking powder together. Add the flour mixture to the butter mixture alternately with the eggs, beating well after each addition. Mix in the vanilla and cream.

4. Spoon the pudding into the prepared mold. Cover the mold with a buttered lid or a buttered double thickness of aluminum foil tightly fitted around the mold.

5. Set the mold on the trivet above the hot water, reduce the heat to medium to keep the water hot but not boiling, and cover the pot. Let the pudding steam for 1 1/2-2 hours, adding hot water as necessary.

6. While the pudding is steaming, prepare the sauce. In a heavy saucepan, combine the brown sugar and butter and simmer for 10 minutes, stirring often. Add the cream. Simmer for 5 minutes, continuing to stir. The

sauce will be a deep caramel color. Remove the saucepan from the heat and blend in the vanilla. Serve warm.

7. Remove the mold to determine if the pudding is done. Remember to use caution when lifting the lid of the steamer. Always use pot holders and direct the release of steam away from yourself. Insert a sharp knife or bamboo skewer into the pudding. If it comes out clean, the pudding is done. If not, continue steaming and test it again. When it is done, allow the pudding to stand, uncovered, for 5 minutes. The pudding might shrink slightly from the sides of the pan, but run a knife carefully around the inside edges of the mold to loosen it further. Place an inverted plate over the mold and, grasping the mold and the plate together, turn them over. The pudding should slide out easily. Slice the pudding at the table, ladle sauce around it, and serve hot.

8. If you wish to freeze the pudding, allow it to cool completely. Then wrap the pudding in aluminum foil and seal it in an airtight freezer bag. To reheat frozen steamed pudding, defrost and steam it in the original mold or wrapped in buttered aluminum foil for 30 minutes or until hot.

Chocolate Cheesecake

MAKES 12-14 SERVINGS

It is said that cheesecakes originated in Greece. Whatever the origin, we are grateful the cheesecake has arrived. Most dessert lovers have well-defined opinions as to what type of cheesecake is best. There are those among us who prefer a light, delicate cheesecake, those that like a dense cake, and those that like it mixed with or topped with fruit. Here is a tall, dense, semisweet chocolate cake that should be served in slivers.

For a change or depending on personal preference, you can substitute milk chocolate for the semisweet chocolate used in the cake. For best results, have all the ingredients at room temperature.

CHOCOLATE CRUMB CRUST
2 cups chocolate cookie crumbs
¼ cup sugar
4 tablespoons (½ stick) unsalted butter, melted and cooled

CAKE
1 pound cream cheese at room temperature, each 8-ounce loaf cut into thirds
1 pound small-curd cottage cheese or pot cheese, drained in a strainer
¾ cup sugar
4 large eggs
3 tablespoons cornstarch
4 tablespoons (½ stick) unsalted butter, melted and cooled

5 ounces semisweet chocolate, melted and cooled
1 cup sour cream
1 teaspoon vanilla extract
2½ tablespoons cream liqueur
Confectioners' sugar, sifted, for sprinkling cake

1. Set a rack in the center of the oven and preheat to 375°F. Butter a 9- or 10-inch springform pan.

2. To prepare the crumb crust, combine the crumbs, sugar, and butter. Press crumb mixture into the bottom and up the sides, ½ to 1 inch, of the springform pan. Refrigerate for 20 minutes.

3. In the large bowl of an electric mixer, blend the cream cheese, drained cottage cheese, and sugar only until smooth. Add the eggs and continue beating on high until incorporated. Add the remaining ingredients except confectioners' sugar. Continue beating until the batter is smooth, about 3–5 minutes. Using a rubber spatula, scrape down the sides of the bowl as necessary. Spoon filling into the chilled crust.

4. Bake the cheesecake for 1 hour and 15 minutes. Lightly touch the cake about 1 inch in from the side. It should spring back lightly. If not, bake for a little longer. Turn off the heat. Leave the cake in the oven to cool for 2 hours. Remove and cool completely. Refrigerate the cheesecake overnight.

5. Run a small sharp knife around the sides of the pan to loosen the cake. Remove the sides but leave the cake on the bottom of the pan. Sprinkle with confectioners' sugar. Cut the cake into thin slices and serve.

State Fair Chocolate Cake with Marshmallow Frosting

MAKES 8–10 SERVINGS

The word *chocolate* comes from the Aztec word *xocoatl* meaning "bitter water." It seems remarkable that such a bitter original product could lead to such an outstanding, wonderfully sweet, rich product.

Most state fairs boast a baking contest. We all have images of generations of proud women who wait all summer for a chance to display their best pies and chocolate layer cakes at the fair. This is our version of such a contender.

CAKE
2¼ cups cake flour
¾ cup unsweetened cocoa
1 teaspoon baking soda
½ teaspoon baking powder
¼ teaspoon salt
¾ cup (1½ sticks) unsalted butter at room temperature
1¾ cups sugar
3 large eggs
1¼ cups buttermilk
1 teaspoon vanilla extract

MARSHMALLOW FROSTING
1½ cups water
1½ cups sugar
Candy thermometer

32 miniature marshmallows or 8 large marshmallows cut into quarters
⅛ teaspoon cream of tartar
3 large egg whites at room temperature

CHOCOLATE DRIZZLE
3 ounces semisweet chocolate, chopped coarse
2 teaspoons unsalted butter

1. Place a rack in the center of the oven and preheat to 350°F. Butter and flour two 9-inch cake pans.

2. Sift the flour, cocoa, baking soda, baking powder, and salt together into a mixing bowl. Set aside.

3. In the large bowl of an electric mixer, beat the butter until light, about 3 minutes. Add the sugar and continue beating until light, about 3 minutes longer. Using a rubber spatula, scrape down the sides of the bowl as needed. Add the eggs, one at a time, beating well to incorporate. Add the flour mixture alternately with the buttermilk, incorporating after each addition. Add the vanilla and mix. Use a spatula to spread the batter evenly into the prepared pans.

4. Bake the cakes for 30–35 minutes or until a bamboo skewer or toothpick inserted in the center comes out dry and clean. Cool the cakes for a few minutes, then loosen them by running a knife around the inside of the pans. Invert the cakes onto a wire rack. Using much care, invert one cake right side up onto the rack. Cool the cakes completely.

5. When the cakes have cooled, prepare the frosting. Put the water in a small heavy saucepan and mix in the sugar. Set the candy thermometer in place. Cook the sugar syrup over medium heat until the temperature reaches 239–240°F.

6. Remove the pan from the heat and stir in the marshmallows and cream of tartar. Stir until the marshmallows are melted and set aside.

7. Beat the egg whites with an electric mixer until stiff but not dry peaks form. With the beaters running, pour the marshmallow mixture in a slow steady stream down the side of the mixing bowl. The marshmallow syrup will become incorporated and whip up to a frothy marshmallow frosting. Cool slightly.

8. While frosting is cooling, melt the chocolate and butter in a microwave or in the top of a double boiler over but not touching simmering water. Mix to blend well. Cool.

9. To frost the cake, first set a layer flat side up on a cake plate. Using a frosting knife or kitchen knife, frost the top of the cake layer. Gently position the remaining layer on top, rounded side up. Frost the top and sides of the cake. Drizzle the chocolate around the edge of the cake, allowing it to drizzle down the sides. Let the frosting set before slicing.

Note: The cake can be baked and wrapped in aluminum foil or plastic wrap for up to 2 days before serving. Store at room temperature. Frost before serving.

Chocolate Chip Sour Cream Coffee Cake

MAKES 12 SERVINGS

Chocolate Chip Sour Cream Coffee Cake is just what the name implies—a dense, rich cake studded with chocolate chips. In addition, the cake has a candied pecan topping. Use either semisweet chips or milk chocolate chips. This cake serves many guests and is a good one to have in your freezer for last-minute company.

TOPPING

½ cup shelled pecans or walnuts, chopped
¼ cup lightly packed light brown sugar
1 teaspoon ground cinnamon
1 tablespoon all-purpose flour

CAKE

2 cups all-purpose flour
1½ teaspoons baking powder
½ teaspoon baking soda
¼ teaspoon salt
¾ cup (1½ sticks) unsalted butter at room temperature
1¼ cups sugar
2 large eggs, separated, at room temperature
1 cup sour cream
1 teaspoon vanilla extract
1¼ cups chocolate morsels
½ cup golden raisins
¼ teaspoon cream of tartar

1. Set a rack in the center of the oven and preheat to 350°F. Butter and flour a Bundt, tube, or springform pan.

2. To prepare topping, mix the pecans or walnuts, brown sugar, cinnamon, and flour together in a small bowl. Set aside.

3. Sift the flour, baking powder, baking soda, and salt together. Set aside.

4. In the large bowl of an electric mixer, beat the butter until light, about 3 minutes. Add 1 cup of the sugar and continue beating until light, about 2 minutes longer. Add the egg yolks and incorporate. Using a rubber spatula, scrape down the sides of the bowl from time to time.

5. Add the flour mixture alternately with the sour cream, incorporating after each addition. Mix in the vanilla, chocolate chips, and raisins.

6. Beat the egg whites until soft peaks form. Sprinkle the egg whites with the cream of tartar and remaining ¼ cup sugar. Continue beating the whites until stiff peaks form.

7. Using a spatula, fold the egg whites into the batter.

8. Sprinkle the topping into the prepared pan and pour the batter over the topping. Bake for 50 minutes or until cake just begins to shrink from the sides of the pan and a bamboo skewer inserted in the center comes out dry and clean. Cool the cake in the pan for 3–5 minutes. Run a small sharp knife around the inside edges of the pan and invert the cake onto a wire rack. Cool completely.

SACHER TORTE—THE LORE

Sacher torte is truly the gastronomic stuff of dreams: a rich chocolate cake base covered with a thick layer of apricot jam and then drenched in a coating of bittersweet chocolate. But this most famous cake in the world has a history and reputation to match its textures and flavors.

The cake was created in 1832 by a 16-year-old Austrian baker, Franz Sacher, who first combined its particular ingredients in their just proportions while working for Prince Metternich, Austria's imperial chancellor. In the next 17 years, Sacher changed jobs many times. But as he went from one noble house to another, he took his recipe with him.

Then, in 1849, Sacher opened a modest hotel and delicatessen and put his cake on the menu, where the general public developed a fondness for it.

Finally, in 1876—27 years later—the Sacher cake began receiving the kudos it deserved, when Franz's son Eduard opened the grand Hotel Sacher and made the torte its culinary logo.

In the next 75 years or so, many restaurants and pastry shops—including the world-famous Demel's in Vienna, Austria—served their version of the Sacher torte. Still, all was well for many years. The Sachers tolerated this bluster, secure in the knowledge that they and only they made the true Sacher torte.

Then one day the Sachers added an innovation: they split the cake into two horizontal layers and added a layer of apricot jam between the two.

Sacher's customers were delighted with this culinary step forward. But Demel's immediately criticized the new version. Demel's insisted that this split and the additional jam were a desecration, not an innovation. And soon Demel's began insisting that only its cake was the *echte*, the genuine article.

Finally, sometime in the 1950s, the Sachers got so angry that they filed a lawsuit in the Viennese courts. Plaintiff Sacher begged the courts to decree, once and for all, that the Sacher Hotel's version was the real thing and that defendant Demel's version was an imitation.

For nine years many lawyers argued about whether the real thing meant one large uncut layer or a layer that was split and filled with additional apricot jam. And then, finally, in June 1962, the judges announced a final decision: only the Sacher Hotel can claim to serve the real Sacher torte.

If this wasn't enough, the judges made an addendum: the split in the middle and the extra layer of jam represented an innovation and not a desecration.

Despite the courts, the people of Vienna have not—to this day—made up their minds. And whether you visit the Sacher Hotel or Demel's for *jause*—the Viennese-style coffee break—you can, if you listen carefully, hear the hushed murmurings of an unresolved clientele.

Sacher Torte

MAKES ONE 10-INCH CAKE OR 12 SERVINGS

Sacher torte recipes claiming to be the original appear in numerous books. The most common one contains 8 egg yolks and 10 egg whites, ¾ cup each of butter and sugar, 6½ ounces of unsweetened chocolate, and a cup of flour.

We have made four changes in the basic recipe: (1) Vanilla is added to accommodate American tastes. (2) Sugar is taken from the recipe and added to the whites so the stiffer meringue that results can be folded more easily into the dense batter. (3) Since the 8- or 9-inch springform usually called for is too small for the batter, we bake the torte in a 10-inch springform. (4) Since American jam is thinner than European jam, we've increased the amount so the top and sides of the torte can be covered generously. If you split the cake in two, add another ¼ cup jam. *Note*: Don't strain or heat the jam before spreading. This makes it too thin.

CAKE
8 large egg yolks
2 teaspoons vanilla extract
¾ cup (1½ sticks) unsalted butter at room temperature
¾ cup sugar
6½ ounces semisweet chocolate, melted (don't use morsels)
1 cup sifted all-purpose flour
10 large egg whites at room temperature
⅛ teaspoon cream of tartar

UNDERCOATING
about ½ cup apricot jam

POURED CHOCOLATE FROSTING

1 cup sugar
½ cup water
Candy thermometer
4½ ounces unsweetened chocolate, chopped
2 tablespoons unsalted butter
1 teaspoon vanilla extract
Hot tap water as needed
1 cup heavy cream, whipped (optional)

1. Set a rack in the center of the oven and preheat to 300°F. Generously grease and flour a 10-inch springform pan. For the cake, beat the egg yolks in the large bowl of an electric mixer until very thick and fluffy, about 1 minute. Add the vanilla and beat again.

2. In a separate bowl, beat the butter until soft and light, about 1 minute. Add 6 tablespoons of the sugar and beat until well combined, about 1 minute.

3. Add the chocolate, then the egg-yolk mixture, beating about 1 minute after each addition. Beat in the flour.

4. Beat the egg whites until they stand in soft peaks. Add the cream of tartar and beat until the whites hold stiff peaks. With the beaters still running, add the remaining 6 tablespoons sugar in a thin stream. Turn off the beaters as soon as the sugar is added.

5. Fold one-quarter of the meringue into the chocolate batter. Fold the remaining meringue into the chocolate mixture.

6. Spoon the batter into the prepared pan. Bake for 1

hour or until a toothpick inserted in the center of the cake comes out clean and dry.

7. Remove the sides of the pan and let the cake sit for 5 minutes. Invert it onto a wire rack and cool. Let the cake sit for 4 hours or more before filling. If the cake is uneven, use a serrated knife to level it.

8. For the filling, spread jam on the top and sides of the cake. (If desired, split the cake in two horizontally and spread additional jam between the layers.) Refrigerate the cake for 1 hour to set the jam.

9. Place the cold cake on a 9-inch cardboard circle. Set the cake on a wire rack over a cookie sheet with raised sides. For the frosting, combine the sugar and water in a heavy-bottomed saucepan, set the candy thermometer in place, and heat to 234°F. Immediately remove the pan from the heat and stir in the chocolate, butter, and vanilla. Mix well with a wire whisk. If the frosting isn't liquid enough to pour easily, whisk in hot water, 2 tablespoons at a time, until the frosting reaches pouring consistency.

10. Quickly tilt the saucepan over the cake and pour the icing over. It will smooth itself out and drip down the sides. Use a rubber spatula to cover empty spots on the sides. Let the cake remain on the rack at room temperature for at least 6 hours and preferably overnight for the icing to set and the cake to ripen.

11. Transfer the cake to a serving platter. Pass a bowl filled with whipped cream at serving time.

Chocolate Pudding and Chocolate Pudding Pie

MAKES 8 SERVINGS

The pleasures of puddings have never diminished, especially in England, where even today the term *pudding* covers a much wider range than we in America would traditionally associate with it. "What's for pudding?" refers to the entire gamut of desserts that follow the main course of an English meal.

Chocolate Pudding is a favorite among hidden treasures of recipes. It has a silky, soothing quality that makes it a classic favorite for all ages.

PUDDING
⅓ cup unsweetened cocoa
½ cup sugar
2½ tablespoons cornstarch
2 cups milk
1 teaspoon vanilla extract

PIECRUST
1¼ cups all-purpose flour
¼ teaspoon salt
6 tablespoons cold vegetable shortening
1 tablespoon cold, unsalted butter
3–6 tablespoons cold water

GARNISH/TOPPING
Sweetened whipped cream
Shaved chocolate (optional)

1. Combine the cocoa, sugar, and cornstarch in a bowl. Mix ¼ cup of the milk into the dry ingredients. Set aside.

2. In a heavy saucepan, scald the remaining milk. Whisk in the cocoa mixture. Stirring often, simmer until the pudding thickens, about 10 minutes.

3. Pour the pudding into a bowl; mix in the vanilla. Cool.

4. To make the piecrust, mix the flour and salt in a bowl. Cut in the shortening and butter with a pastry knife or use a food processor fitted with a steel blade. Process until the dough resembles coarse crumbs. Sprinkle the dough with water by the tablespoon, mixing until a smooth, not soggy, dough is formed. Gather the dough into a ball and cover with plastic wrap. Refrigerate for 30 minutes before using.

5. Roll out the dough to a 10-inch circle on a lightly floured surface or use a pastry cloth. Place the dough in a 9-inch pie plate, patting it with your fingers until it extends just past the edges of the pie plate. Firm down the edges of the crust using the tines of a fork. Prick the crust in several places and set a sheet of aluminum foil over it. Press the foil down against the dough to help the crust keep its shape during baking. Cover the foil with pie weights or dry beans. Bake the crust in the center of a preheated 475°F oven for 10 minutes. Remove the foil and weights. Bake the crust for 5 minutes longer. Remove the crust from the oven and cool.

6. Spoon the cooled pudding into individual dessert dishes or into a cooled piecrust and chill until set. To serve, cover the pie with sweetened whipped cream. If you're serving pudding alone, you can garnish it with sweetened whipped cream and/or shaved chocolate.

Southern Chocolate Layer Cake

MAKES 8 SERVINGS

Imagine a moist chocolate cake with a praline dried fruit filling and a sour cream frosting. There you have it: Southern Chocolate Layer Cake.

CAKE

1¾ cups all-purpose flour
½ cup unsweetened cocoa
1¼ teaspoons baking soda
¼ teaspoon salt
4 tablespoons (½ stick) unsalted butter at room temperature
1¼ cups granulated sugar
2 large eggs
½ cup vegetable oil
¾ cup buttermilk
1 teaspoon vanilla extract

PRALINE FRUIT FILLING

1 cup half-and-half
¼ cup firmly packed light brown sugar
1 tablespoon cornstarch
½ cup golden raisins
¼ cup chopped dried figs
¼ cup chopped pitted dates
1 teaspoon vanilla extract
½ cup chopped pecans

SOUR CREAM FROSTING

¼ pound (⅔ cup) semisweet chocolate morsels
4 tablespoons (½ stick) unsalted butter
½ cup sour cream
1 teaspoon vanilla extract
2¾ cups confectioners' sugar, sifted

1. Butter and flour two 8-inch round cake pans. Set a rack in the center of the oven and preheat to 350°F.

2. Sift the flour, cocoa, baking soda, and salt together. Set aside.

3. In the large bowl of an electric mixer, beat the butter until light, about 3 minutes. Add the granulated sugar and continue beating until light. Add the eggs, one at a time, beating well to incorporate. Add the oil and beat until smooth. Add the flour mixture alternately with the buttermilk in three batches, beating well after each addition. Scrape down the sides of the bowl with a rubber spatula as necessary. Mix in the vanilla.

4. Using a rubber spatula, scrape the batter evenly into the prepared cake pans. Bake the cake for 25–30 minutes or until the cake just begins to shrink from the sides of the pan and a bamboo skewer or toothpick inserted in the center comes out dry and clean. Cool the cake for 5 minutes. Loosen the cake by running a knife around the edges. Invert the cake onto a wire rack and cool. Carefully invert one layer right side up.

5. To prepare the filling, pour the half-and-half and brown sugar into a small heavy saucepan. Simmer for 4 minutes, stirring occasionally. Remove 1 tablespoon of the liquid and whisk in a cup with the cornstarch. Return to the pan and stir to combine. Mix in the fruit

and continue cooking for 5-7 minutes over medium heat, until the filling thickens. It will be a light brown color. Remove from the heat and stir in the vanilla and nuts.

6. Spread the cooled filling over the bottom flat layer of cake. Position the top rounded layer over the cake. Make the frosting.

7. Melt the chocolate and butter in a small glass dish in the microwave or in a heavy saucepan or in the top of a double boiler over but not touching simmering water. Stir to combine. Using an electric mixer or a food processor fitted with the steel blade, blend in the sour cream, vanilla, and confectioners' sugar and process until combined. The frosting should be spreading consistency. If not, add sour cream by the tablespoon. With a knife, spread the frosting over the top and sides of the cake.

Warm Chocolate Chip Butter Cookies

MAKES 32 2-INCH COOKIES

These cookies can be served at room temperature, but they're especially delicious warm. To be sure they're warm when you want to serve them, place the unbaked cookies on cookie sheets and refrigerate, covered, until 30 minutes before serving time. Give the cookies a few minutes to come to room temperature before putting them in the oven.

Note: All cookies burn easily, especially when you're paying attention to guests in the other room. Watch them often during baking.

1 cup (2 sticks) unsalted butter, softened
¾ cup lightly packed dark brown sugar
1¾ cups all-purpose flour
½ teaspoon vanilla extract
⅔ cup or more semisweet chocolate morsels
Confectioners' sugar (optional)

1. Set a rack in the center of the oven and preheat to 325°F. Beat the butter and brown sugar in the large bowl of an electric mixer until well mixed. Add the flour and vanilla and beat again. Stir in the chocolate morsels.

2. Divide the dough into four equal-sized pieces. Divide each piece into eight balls. Place the balls on an ungreased baking sheet and flatten each with your palm. Leave 2 inches of space between flattened cookies.

Examine the cookies to make sure each has enough chocolate morsels. Add morsels as needed.

3. Bake for 18–20 minutes or until lightly browned. Transfer the hot cookies to a wire rack with a spatula. Cool for a minute or two, then transfer to a serving plate. Sift confectioners' sugar over the tops if desired. Serve immediately, while warm.

'Twill make Old women Young and Fresh;
Create New Motions of the Flesh,
And cause them long for you know what,
If they but taste of Chocolate.

From *A Curious History of the Nature and Quality of Chocolate* by James Wadsworth, 16th century

Chocolate Baltimore Cake

MAKES TWO 10-INCH LAYERS
OR 12 SERVINGS

Owen Wister wrote his novel *Lady Baltimore* in 1906, following a visit to Charleston, where he tasted this delicious cake. Haunted by its flavor, he surely would have written a sequel if he could have tasted our chocolate version.

Note: Since the raisins and figs must be steeped in sherry for at least 2 hours, you may want to do step 5 before you bake the layers.

CAKE
1 cup (2 sticks) unsalted butter at room temperature
1½ cups lightly packed dark brown sugar
2½ cups sifted cake flour
½ cup sifted unsweetened cocoa
1 tablespoon baking powder
1 cup milk
1½ teaspoons vanilla extract
6 large egg whites at room temperature
⅛ teaspoon cream of tartar
⅓ cup granulated sugar

SHERRY, FRUIT, AND PECAN FROSTING
1½ cups raisins
10 dried figs, cut into small pieces with scissors
1 cup or more dry sherry
1½ cups granulated sugar
¾ cup water

2 teaspoons light corn syrup
Candy thermometer
3 large egg whites at room temperature
⅛ teaspoon cream of tartar
1½ cups coarsely chopped pecans

1. Set a rack in the center of the oven and preheat to 350°F. Liberally grease and flour two 10-inch round cake pans.

2. In the large bowl of an electric mixer, beat the butter until soft. Add the brown sugar and beat until well combined. Beat in the cake flour, cocoa, and baking powder alternately with the milk and vanilla, beginning and ending with flour. Beat until very well mixed.

3. Beat the egg whites until they hold soft peaks. Add the cream of tartar and beat until stiff. With the beaters running, add the granulated sugar in a thin stream. Turn the beaters off as soon as the sugar is added.

4. Fold the meringue into the chocolate mixture. Divide the batter evenly between the prepared pans. Bake for about 30 minutes or until a toothpick inserted in the center of the layers comes out clean and dry. Turn the layers out onto wire racks to cool.

5. For the frosting, place the raisins, fig pieces, and enough sherry to immerse them in a plastic bag and secure with a twister seal. Place the bag in a small bowl. Let them steep for 2–3 hours, turning occasionally.

6. Combine the granulated sugar, water, and corn syrup in a heavy-bottomed saucepan. Set a candy thermometer in place and cook without stirring to 234°F.

7. While the syrup cooks, beat the egg whites until they hold soft peaks. Beat in the cream of tartar. Continue beating until stiff.

8. When the syrup reaches 234°F, pour it in a thin stream over the egg whites with the beaters running. Continue beating until the mixture is stiff.

9. Strain the raisin and fig mixture and discard the soaking liquid. Stir the raisins, figs, and pecans into the frosting.

10. Cover the edges of a serving plate with strips of wax paper. Place a cake layer on the plate and cover thickly with frosting. Place the second layer on top and cover the sides and top thickly with frosting. Allow to set for 1 hour. Carefully pull out the wax paper strips.

"I shall also advise my fair readers to be in a particular manner careful how they meddle with romances, chocolate, novels and the like inflamers, which I look upon as very dangerous. . . ."

From *The Spectator* by
Joseph Addison, 1712

Chocolate Kentucky Bourbon Pecan Cake

MAKES ONE 10-INCH TUBE CAKE
OR 16 SERVINGS

This delicious cake is a chocolate version of the famous Kentucky Bourbon Pecan Cake. No one is certain when the Kentucky Bourbon Pecan Cake first appeared on the Christmas scene, but most southerners agree that it's delicious—an example of southern holiday cake making at its traditional best.

But we think our chocolate version is so good that it should be made at any time of the year, including summer. In fact, we can't imagine a better accompaniment to iced tea.

The cake will keep for several weeks when doused with bourbon, wrapped in a bourbon-soaked cloth, and enclosed in a covered tin or wrapped in aluminum foil and refrigerated.

1½ cups raisins
1⅓ cups good-quality bourbon
½ cup unsweetened cocoa, worked through a strainer
2 teaspoons baking powder
1 teaspoon baking soda
1 teaspoon nutmeg
1½ cups (3 sticks) unsalted butter at room temperature
1 pound dark brown sugar
6 large eggs

⅔ cup red glacé cherries, halved
3 cups coarsely chopped pecans
1 cup pecan halves
3½ cups sifted all-purpose flour
Confectioners' sugar

1. Set a rack in the center of the oven and preheat to 300°F. Grease a 10-inch tube pan, line it (including the center column) with baking parchment or brown paper and liberally grease the paper.

2. Place the raisins in a bowl, cover with 1 cup of the bourbon, and steep while you continue with the recipe. Mix the cocoa, baking powder, baking soda, and nutmeg in a bowl. With a wooden spoon, work the cocoa mixture through a strainer onto a sheet of wax paper or into a bowl; set aside.

3. In the large bowl of an electric mixer, cream the butter, add the brown sugar, and beat about 1 minute or until well mixed. Add the eggs, one at a time, mixing well after each addition. Add the cocoa mixture to the batter and beat well. Lift the raisins from the bourbon, squeeze lightly, and mix with cherries, chopped pecans, and pecan halves. Measure out ½ cup of the flour and toss with the raisin mixture.

4. Measure the bourbon remaining in the bowl and add water to make 1⅓ cups liquid. Add the remaining 3 cups flour and the bourbon/water alternately to the batter, beating well after each addition.

5. Stir the raisin mixture into the batter. Let the batter rest at room temperature for 15 minutes. Spoon the batter into the prepared pan and even the top with a spatula. Bake for 2 hours and 20 minutes or until a cake tester inserted deep in the center comes out clean and

dry. Remove the cake from the oven and set on a wire rack to cool in the pan. When cool, remove from the pan.

6. Pour the remaining ⅓ cup bourbon into the cracks and over the top of the cake. Wrap in a bourbon-soaked cloth, then in aluminum foil, and refrigerate. Allow to ripen overnight before cutting. At serving time, sift confectioners' sugar over the top.

Fiona Merriweather's Chocolate Tea

When we received an invitation to one of the famed English afternoon teas hosted by our friend Fiona Merriweather, we were thrilled to discover that the theme was chocolate, in our honor. And we liked the idea so much that we decided to include a chocolate tea in this book.

First we asked Fiona for her chocolate spread recipe. Then we chose chocolate classics from several different countries so our tea would have an international chocolate theme.

Along with her chocolate spread recipe, Fiona gave us a few words of advice about hosting a tea. "No more than eight and no fewer than five compatible—and unhurried—people make for a successful tea," she says. "And although your tea may be chocolate in nature, be sure to include a couple of savories. And try also to serve something chilled, something warm, and something at room temperature along with the hot tea."

Our menu suggestions include the following:

Chilled watercress, Stilton, and smoked salmon finger sandwiches

•

Mistress Merriweather's Chocolate Spread (recipe follows) at room temperature with warm French bread slices

•

Hot toasted slices of Brioche with Chocolate Chips (recipe follows) with room-temperature butter or cream cheese

•

Slices of Chocolate Chip Kugelhopf with Bittersweet Glaze (recipe follows), either at room temperature or lightly toasted

•

Four-cookie platter holding Chocolate Kourambiethes, Double Chocolate Sugar Cookies, Sacher Cookies, and Chocolate Madeleines (recipes follow)

•

Caramel-Frosted Chocolate Cake (recipe follows)

•

Along with the tea, cream, milk, sugar, and lemon, we suggest serving a pot of our delicious Hot Chocolate (see Index)

Mistress Merriweather's Chocolate Spread

MAKES ABOUT 1⅔ CUPS

"Never eat chocolate without bread, young lady! Very bad for the interior, very bad. . . ."

A French doctor's advice to
food writer M. F. K. Fisher,
from her book *Serve It Forth.*

The chocolate and bread combination is popular throughout Europe. French children eat *pain au chocolat*—little breads stuffed with chocolate. Spanish and Belgian children eat chocolate sandwiches; Viennese and Italian children slather their bread with a commercially available chocolate spread.

In America, college students are beginning to buy jars of chocolate spread made with hazelnuts, cocoa, and oil.

Fiona Merriweather has graciously consented to share her chocolate spread recipe with us. "My children love it," she says. "But it's equally popular among adults at afternoon tea."

*½ pound finest English milk chocolate or dark sweet chocolate (*not *semisweet or bittersweet)*
2 ounces roasted salted cashews (just under ½ cup)
½ cup (1 stick) unsalted butter at room temperature
2 tablespoons fine brandy or fruit-flavored liqueur

French bread, raisin toast, or commercial English biscuits

1. Process the chocolate to a paste in a food processor. Transfer the chocolate to a medium-size bowl. Process the cashews to a paste in a food processor.

2. Add the chocolate paste to the cashew paste in the food processor along with the butter and brandy. Process until a smooth paste results. Transfer the spread to a small crock or serving bowl. Cover and refrigerate.

3. One hour before serving time, remove the crock from the refrigerator to bring the spread to room temperature and soften it. Stir in additional brandy or liqueur if desired. Serve with French bread, raisin toast, or English biscuits.

"Caramels are only a fad. Chocolate is a permanent thing. I'm going to make chocolate."

Milton Snavely Hershey's
comment to a friend at
the Chicago Exposition,
1893

Brioche with Chocolate Chips

MAKES ONE 9″ × 5″ LOAF OR 6–8 SERVINGS

We originally wanted to use this bread as an accompaniment to Fiona Merriweather's Chocolate Spread (preceding recipe). But it turned out to be so good that we decided it should be eaten by itself.

⅓ cup warm (110–120°F) tap water
1 ¼-ounce package rapid-rise active dry yeast
⅛ teaspoon ground ginger
3 tablespoons plus 1 teaspoon sugar
⅔ cup unsalted butter at room temperature
4 large eggs
3 cups all-purpose flour, sifted
½ cup semisweet or milk chocolate morsels
1 large egg yolk
2 teaspoons water

1. Place the warm water in the large bowl of an electric mixer and sprinkle the yeast over it. Add the ginger and 1 teaspoon of the sugar. Let sit for 15 minutes or until the yeast begins to foam.

2. Add the remaining 3 tablespoons sugar along with the butter and eggs. Beat for a moment. Then add 2 cups of the flour. Beat for 3–4 minutes at low speed. Add the remaining flour and beat for another 2 minutes. The dough will be very sticky.

3. Press a large plastic bag lightly over the batter. Wet a kitchen towel and wring it out tightly. Drape the towel over the top of the bowl. Set the bowl in a warm

place and allow to rise until double in bulk, about 45-60 minutes.

4. Punch the dough down and rearrange the plastic bag on top. Drape the towel over the bag again. Place in the refrigerator until double in bulk, about 60-75 minutes.

5. Liberally grease a 9″ × 5″ bread pan. Knead the chocolate morsels into the dough. Press the dough into the bottom of the prepared pan. Cover the dough lightly with the plastic bag and set in a warm place for 1 hour or until the dough has doubled in bulk.

6. Set a rack in the center of the oven and preheat to 350°F. Combine the egg yolk with 2 teaspoons water and use a pastry brush to brush the top of the brioche lightly. Bake for 20 minutes. Cover the top lightly with foil and continue baking for 25-30 minutes, a total of 45-50 minutes.

7. Turn the brioche out of the pan and allow to cool on a wire rack. Eat warm or at room temperature. Serve with a crock of room-temperature butter. Brioche is also delicious toasted. Store in a plastic bag secured with a twister seal.

Chocolate Chip Kugelhopf with Bittersweet Glaze

MAKES 12 SERVINGS

The failed Turkish invasion of Vienna in the 17th century was felt even in the pastry. The shape of the Kugelhopf cake pan represents the turbans worn by the sultan. This is a light yeast cake with tiny chocolate chips, orange peel, and currants, glazed with bittersweet chocolate. Kugelhopf pans are available at gourmet shops. You can substitute an 8-cup ring mold or baking pan.

CAKE
1 ¼-ounce package active dry yeast
⅓ cup milk, scalded and cooled to about 110°F
½ cup (1 stick) butter at room temperature
½ cup sugar
2 large eggs at room temperature
2¼ cups all-purpose flour, sifted
¼ teaspoon salt
½ cup dried currants
2 tablespoons dark rum
1 cup miniature chocolate morsels
⅓ cup chopped candied orange peel
¼ cup ground almonds

BITTERSWEET CHOCOLATE GLAZE
2 ounces unsweetened chocolate, coarsely chopped
3 tablespoons heavy cream

1. Set a rack in the center of the oven. Butter a Kugelhopf or other suitable baking pan.

2. Sprinkle the yeast over the warm milk, stir lightly, and set aside for 10–15 minutes, until the yeast foams.

3. In the large bowl of an electric mixer, beat the butter and sugar together until light. Mix in the eggs, one at a time, beating well after each addition, about 1-2 minutes.

4. Mix in the flour, salt, and yeast. The dough will be soft. Turn it into a clean bowl, cover with a clean kitchen towel reserved for this purpose, and let the dough rise in a warm, draft-free area until it has doubled in bulk, about 1 hour and 15 minutes.

5. While the dough is rising, put the currants in a small bowl and sprinkle with rum. Let the currants stand until the dough has risen. Drain the currants and mix them into the dough along with the chocolate morsels, orange peel, and almonds. Put the dough in the prepared pan and cover lightly with a kitchen towel. Let the dough rise again until it reaches the top of the pan, about 1 hour and 15 minutes.

6. Preheat the oven to 350°F. Position the cake in the center of the rack and bake for 40 minutes or until the cake springs back when touched and is golden brown. Let the cake stand on a rack for 5 minutes. Run a small sharp knife around the inside rim of the pan. Invert the cake and cool on a wire rack.

7. While the cake is cooling, prepare the glaze. In a small heavy saucepan, heat the chocolate with the cream over low heat, stirring often until the chocolate has melted and the mixture is smooth. Cool slightly.

8. Brush away any crumbs from the cake and drizzle the glaze over the top and outer edge, allowing the glaze to run down the sides and into the crevices on the sides of the cake.

HANNON'S BEST CHOCOLATE

Marked upon each cake J.H.N.
Warranted pure and ground exceeding fine.
Where may be had any Quantity, from 50wt. to a ton, for Cash or Cocoa, at his Mills in Milton.
N.B. If the Chocolate does not prove good, the Money will be returned.

Advertisement for the Hannon Chocolate Company, 1777, the oldest chocolate company in the United States; today it's known as the Walter Baker Company.

Chocolate Kourambiethes

MAKES 32 2-INCH CRESCENTS

Kourambiethes—those classic Greek butter cookies—are formulated at the breaking point of richness. They're so soft they must be lifted and bitten with care, or they'll splinter before you even get them to your lips.

I was introduced to this cookie many years ago by a Greek boyfriend who purposely didn't tell me how to eat them. When I picked up the first one and it splintered all over my sweater, he laughed teasingly and said, "I just wanted to see if you had a Greek somewhere in your ancestry; if you had, you'd have known how to eat kourambiethes by instinct. We Greeks store this knowledge in our DNA."

Greek bakeries display these cookies on trays, where they're so thickly coated with confectioners' sugar that the cookie can barely be seen. This sugar coating is a necessary part of the cookie's flavor and character, since only a little sugar goes into the recipe itself.

We've created an intense chocolate version of these cookies that retains the softness, richness, and splintery quality of the original. We planned for them to accompany our Hot Chocolate (see Index), but they're delicious any way you serve them.

1 cup (2 sticks) unsalted butter at room temperature
6 tablespoons sifted confectioners' sugar
⅔ cup sifted unsweetened cocoa
1 large egg yolk

1¼ teaspoons vanilla extract
1¼ cups all-purpose flour, sifted
1 cup chopped pecans
⅔ cup confectioners' sugar

1. Set a rack in the center of the oven and preheat to 350°F. In the large bowl of an electric mixer, beat the butter until light, about 1 minute. Add the sifted 6 tablespoons of confectioners' sugar and cocoa and beat until blended. Beat in the egg yolk and vanilla. Beat in the flour until everything is very well combined. Stir in the pecans. Cover the bowl and refrigerate for 1 hour or until the dough is firm enough to work with.

2. Divide the dough in half, then into quarters. Form each quarter into 9 crescents, each about 2 inches long, and place on nonstick cookie sheets (or line baking sheets with cooking parchment). Bake the cookies for 10 minutes. Let cool on the baking sheet.

3. *Carefully* transfer the cookies to a serving platter. Sift the ⅔ cup confectioners' sugar over the cookies. The sugar coating should be so thick that the cookies can barely be seen.

Double Chocolate Sugar Cookies

MAKES 22-24 COOKIES

Three-inch chocolate sugar cookies topped with ground pistachio nuts and drizzled with chocolate make a marvelous addition to your cookie recipe collection.

COOKIES
2½ cups all-purpose flour
2¼ tablespoons Dutch cocoa
2 teaspoons baking powder
¼ teaspoon baking soda
¼ teaspoon salt
½ cup (1 stick) unsalted butter at room temperature
1 cup sugar, plus extra for sprinkling cookies
2 large eggs
1 teaspoon vanilla extract
¾ cup ground pistachios or other nuts

TOPPING
¼ pound semisweet chocolate
1 teaspoon vegetable oil

1. Set a rack in the center of the oven and preheat to 375°F. Lightly butter a cookie sheet.

2. Sift the flour, cocoa, baking powder, baking soda, and salt together. Set aside.

3. In the large bowl of an electric mixer, cream the butter and 1 cup sugar together until light. Using a rubber spatula, scrape down the sides of the bowl as

necessary. Add the eggs, beating well. Gradually add the flour mixture. Blend well. Mix in the vanilla.

4. Gather the dough together into a ball, cover with aluminum foil, and refrigerate 1½–2 hours.

5. Divide the dough in half. Use a pastry cloth and rolling pin sleeve (available at gourmet shops and hardware stores). Sprinkle sugar lightly over the pastry cloth and roll out half of the dough until about ¼ inch thick. Use a 2½- or 3-inch cookie cutter or glass to cut out cookies. With a spatula, lift them onto the prepared cookie sheet about 1½ inches apart. Sprinkle the cookies with sugar and pistachio nuts. Gently press the nuts into the cookies.

6. Bake the cookies for 8–9 minutes or until the edges are just beginning to brown. Transfer the cookies to a wire rack to cool.

7. Melt the chocolate in a microwave for 2–3 minutes or in the top of a double boiler over but not touching simmering water. Mix in the oil and stir until the chocolate is smooth. Spoon the chocolate into a small plastic bag or use a pointed paper cup. Force the chocolate into one corner of the bag. With scissors, cut a tiny snip off the bag. At this corner, gently force the chocolate in a free-form design over cookies. Let the chocolate harden. Store in an airtight container for up to 2 weeks.

Sacher Cookies

MAKES ABOUT 54 DOUBLE COOKIES

COOKIES
1 cup (2 sticks) unsalted butter at room temperature
½ cup sugar
1¼ cups (5 ounces) blanched almonds, ground
2 tablespoons unsweetened cocoa
Scant 2 cups all-purpose flour

FILLING
½ cup strained raspberry jam

CHOCOLATE FROSTING
1 cup sugar
½ cup water
Candy thermometer
4½ ounces unsweetened chocolate, coarsely chopped
2 tablespoons unsalted butter
1 teaspoon vanilla extract
1 tablespoon ground almonds (optional)

1. Set a rack in the center of the oven and preheat to 300°F. Grease cookie sheets. For the cookie dough, mix the butter, sugar, almonds, cocoa, and flour together with fingers to form a dough. Roll out the dough ⅛ inch thick between sheets of wax paper. Cut out 2-inch circles with a cookie cutter or glass and place them on the prepared cookie sheets.

2. Bake the cookies for 10–15 minutes, watching them carefully so they don't burn. Let the cookies cool on a baking sheet until firm. Transfer to a wire rack to cool.

3. For the filling, press the jam through a strainer with a wooden spoon. Discard the seeds.

4. Spread about ¼ teaspoon jam on half of the cookies. Top each with another cookie.

5. For the frosting, mix the sugar and water in a heavy-bottomed saucepan and set a candy thermometer in place. Cook until the syrup reaches 234°F, immediately remove from the heat, and stir in the chocolate and butter. Mix well, then stir in the vanilla. The frosting should be thin enough to spread easily. If thick, stir in hot tap water a spoonful at a time.

6. Spread a thin layer of frosting on top of the cookie pairs. Add additional hot water as needed throughout the frosting process. Sprinkle ground almonds over the frosting if desired.

Chocolate Madeleines

MAKES 22-24 COOKIES

Madeleine is a girl's name in France, but it is also the name of a small, light, delicate, spongy shell-shaped cake that is eaten like a cookie. Madeleines are baked in a special pan (available at gourmet stores) that gives them the scalloplike indentations of a shell.

It was retasting tea and madeleines that stimulated French author Marcel Proust to recall his boyhood in the town of Combray and then write about it in his *Remembrance of Things Past.* But we suspect that, had he tasted our chocolate version of this little French cake, he would have spent his time eating madeleines rather than writing about them.

4 large eggs at room temperature
¾ cup sugar
10 tablespoons unsalted butter
1 ounce semisweet chocolate, coarsely chopped
1 cup all-purpose flour
3 tablespoons unsweetened cocoa
½ teaspoon salt
6 ounces white chocolate, coarsely chopped

1. Set a rack in the center of the oven and preheat to 350°F. Grease a madeleine pan.

2. Beat the eggs in the large bowl of an electric mixer until light, about 3 minutes. Sprinkle the sugar over the eggs and continue beating until the sugar is absorbed.

3. While you beat the eggs, melt the butter and semisweet chocolate in a small glass dish in a microwave or in the top of a double boiler over but not touching simmering water. Stir the chocolate mixture to combine.

4. Sift the flour, cocoa, and salt together. Mix the flour mixture and melted chocolate alternately into the batter.

5. Spoon the batter into the prepared molds, two-thirds full, about 1 heaped teaspoon of batter. Bake the madeleines for 12-14 minutes or until a toothpick inserted in the center of a cookie comes out clean and dry. The cookies will spring back when touched gently. Cool the cookies in the pan on a rack for 10 minutes. The cookies will begin to shrink from the ends of the pan and spring back to the touch. Remove them from the pan and cool completely on a wire rack. Repeat until all the cookies have been baked.

6. Melt the white chocolate in a small glass dish in a microwave or in the top of a double boiler over but not touching simmering water. Stir the chocolate until smooth. Hold a madeleine by the larger end and dip it into the chocolate to about ½-¾ inch. Drip excess chocolate back into the pan and set the cookie on a sheet of wax paper to dry. Repeat with the remaining cookies, set them decoratively on a tray, and serve. Store in an airtight container.

Caramel-Frosted Chocolate Cake

MAKES TWO 9-INCH LAYERS OR 8 SERVINGS

Caramel fudge is an elegant foil to a good quality chocolate cake, both visually and gastronomically. Although both cake and frosting are very delicious by themselves, the combination is unbeatable.

CAKE
1 cup (2 sticks) unsalted butter at room temperature
1 cup lightly packed dark brown sugar
3 large eggs, separated, at room temperature
2½ ounces unsweetened chocolate, melted
1½ teaspoons vanilla extract
Scant 2 cups sifted cake flour
1½ teaspoons baking powder
⅔ cup milk
⅛ teaspoon cream of tartar
¼ cup granulated sugar

CARAMEL FUDGE FROSTING
3 cups lightly packed light or dark brown sugar or a combination
1 cup buttermilk
Candy thermometer
2 tablespoons unsalted butter
Several tablespoons milk as needed

1. Set a rack in the center of the oven and preheat to 325°F. Liberally grease and flour two 9-inch round cake pans. In the large bowl of an electric mixer, beat the

butter and brown sugar until well mixed, about 1 minute. Beat in the egg yolks, then the melted chocolate and vanilla.

2. Add the flour and baking powder alternately with the milk, beginning and ending with flour.

3. Beat the egg whites until they hold soft peaks. Add the cream of tartar and beat until stiff. With the beaters running, add the granulated sugar in a thin stream. Stop beating as soon as the sugar is incorporated.

4. Spoon the batter over the meringue and fold together lightly but thoroughly until no unmixed patches remain. Divide the batter evenly between the prepared pans. Bake for 25–30 minutes or until a toothpick inserted in the center comes out clean and dry. Let sit in the pans on wire racks for 5 minutes, then invert onto the racks to cool.

5. For the frosting, combine the brown sugar and buttermilk in a heavy-bottomed saucepan. Set a candy thermometer in place and simmer over medium heat until the mixture reaches 238°F. Quickly set the pan bottom in a bowl of cool water to halt cooking.

6. Transfer the frosting to an electric mixer bowl and add the butter. Beat until the frosting cools and is thick enough to spread. If it resembles a glaze, it needs more beating.

7. Spread some frosting thinly on one cake layer. Place the second layer over the frosting. Spread the remaining frosting over the top and sides of the cake. The frosting will thicken as you use it. Use a wire whisk to incorporate milk, one spoonful at a time, to thin it as needed.

Pots de Crème au Chocolat

MAKES 6 SERVINGS

Do you want to make an easy elegant dessert? Then try Pots de Crème au Chocolat. You can serve these with a mound of sweetened whipped cream, chopped nuts, and/or shaved chocolate.

There are decorative cups designed especially for this dessert, but they're hard to find. Footed glasses or small tea cups can be used instead.

CHOCOLATE CREAM
½ cup half-and-half or milk
2 ounces unsweetened chocolate, chopped
1 teaspoon unsalted butter
¾ cup confectioners' sugar, sifted
1 teaspoon vanilla extract
2 large egg yolks
1 cup heavy cream

SWEETENED WHIPPED CREAM
½ cup heavy cream
3 tablespoons granulated sugar
¾ teaspoon vanilla extract

1. In a small heavy saucepan or in the top of a double boiler over but not touching simmering water, heat the half-and-half, chocolate, and butter. Whisk often until the chocolate has melted. Stir in the confectioners' sugar and whisk until incorporated. Remove from the heat and blend in the vanilla.

2. Place the egg yolks in a bowl and slowly whisk in

the chocolate so as not to curdle the eggs. Return the mixture to a heavy saucepan. Simmer, whisking almost constantly, until the mixture thickens, about 1-1½ minutes. Remove the chocolate from the heat and quickly transfer to a bowl. Chill.

3. Beat the heavy cream until firm peaks form. Fold the whipped cream into the chilled chocolate.

4. Spoon the cream into small teacups, custard cups, or footed glasses. Chill until firm, about 1 hour.

5. When you're ready to serve, whip the chilled cream until soft peaks form. Sprinkle the cream with granulated sugar and continue beating until firm peaks form. Mix in the vanilla. Mound a dollop of sweetened whipped cream over the Pots de Crème. Serve chilled.

Dutch Flourless Chocolate Cake

MAKES 8-10 SERVINGS

Did you ever have the desire to eat a bowl full of cake batter? Maybe not, but many children, and more adults, know the pleasure of eating the batter left on the insides of a cake bowl. This recipe is adapted from a traditional Dutch recipe called Fallen Cake. The name derives from the fact that a portion of the batter is reserved, and the cake falls or collapses after baking. The resulting cavity is filled with the reserved batter. This produces a cake with two densities and an extraordinary richness and texture for a flourless cake. (If eating raw egg bothers you, do not reserve any uncooked batter. Cook all batter at the same time.)

CAKE
6 ounces bittersweet chocolate, chopped
3 tablespoons strong brewed coffee
6 large eggs, separated, at room temperature
⅔ cup plus 6 tablespoons sugar
¼ teaspoon salt
1 cup heavy cream
6 tablespoons sugar
1 teaspoon vanilla

1. Set a rack in the center of the oven and preheat to 350°F. Butter a 9-inch springform pan.

2. Melt the chocolate along with the coffee in a glass bowl in the microwave or in the top of a double boiler over but not touching simmering water. Stir the chocolate until smooth. Cool.

3. While the chocolate is cooling, beat the egg whites in the large bowl of an electric mixer until soft peaks form. Sprinkle the 6 tablespoons sugar over the egg whites and beat to incorporate. Continue beating until stiff peaks form. Set aside.

4. In a clean bowl of the electric mixer, beat the yolks with the ⅔ cup sugar on medium speed until thick and light. Beat in the cooled chocolate and salt. Remove the bowl from the mixer and with a rubber spatula fold in one-third of the egg whites. Then fold in the remaining whites. Place a third of the batter in a small bowl; cover and refrigerate. Pour the remaining batter into the prepared pan.

5. Bake the cake for 25 minutes, turn off the oven, and leave the cake in the unopened oven for 5 minutes. The center of the cake will fall, and a rim will form at the edges. The cake will be about 1–1½ inches high.

6. While hot, run a small sharp knife around the edges of the cake, remove the springform sides and let the cake cool on a wire rack. When completely cooled, spread the refrigerated batter carefully over the indentation of the cake. Refrigerate for 1 hour.

7. When ready to serve, slowly whip the cream until it begins to thicken. Sprinkle the remaining 6 tablespoons sugar into the cream and beat until soft peaks form. Mix in the vanilla. Either dollop sweetened whipped cream over the cake or place the whipped cream in a pastry bag fitted with a star tip and decorate the cake.

Hot Fudge Sundae, Ice Cream Soda, and Egg Cream

Ice cream itself is said to have been a creation of the ancient Chinese, probably as a soft paste of rice and milk mixed with mountain snow. However, mankind had to wait nearly 3,000 years before the invention of the delectable ice cream sundae. This seems a shame and a waste of valuable time.

While the exact origin of the sundae is unknown, H. L. Mencken suggested a plausible theory in his work *The American Language*. Sometime during the 1890s a customer in an ice cream parlor in Two Rivers, Wisconsin, requested that his ice cream be topped with chocolate syrup. The proprietor, one E. C. Berners, complied, and one of America's favorite dessert dishes was born.

A variant story credits the origin of the sundae to the owner of a pharmacy/soda fountain in Evanston, Illinois, in the 19th century. At the time a favorite weekend treat was the ice cream soda. However, because the "blue laws" prohibited the consumption of carbonated beverages on Sunday, this enterprising individual, name unknown to history, topped ice cream with syrup and created a "dry" version of the ice cream soda.

While a spelling lapse may account for the "sundae," it is more likely the dish was named after the day on which soda was banned and spelled creatively so as not to be sacrilegious.

Anyway, the hot fudge sundae is a wonderful combination of "fire and ice." Try our Chocolate Ice Cream in place of vanilla for the classic treat.

CHOCOLATE ICE CREAM
(Makes about 1½ quarts; 8 servings)

1 cup milk
6 ounces semisweet chocolate, coarsely chopped
4 large egg yolks
1 cup sugar
1 teaspoon ground cinnamon
2 teaspoons vanilla extract
3 cups heavy cream

HOT FUDGE SAUCE
(Makes about 2 cups)

⅔ cup sugar
½ cup unsweetened cocoa, sifted
¾–1 cup heavy cream
⅓ cup light corn syrup
6 tablespoons unsalted butter
1 teaspoon vanilla extract

Sweetened whipped cream (see Index)
1 cup chopped peanuts, pecans, or other nuts
8 maraschino cherries

1. For the ice cream, pour the milk into the top of a double boiler over but not touching simmering water or into a heavy saucepan over medium heat. Add the chocolate and continue cooking until the milk is scalded and the chocolate has melted, stirring occasionally until blended. Cool.

2. In the large bowl of an electric mixer, beat the egg yolks until light. Add the sugar and continue beating until light, about 4 minutes. In a slow, steady stream, beat in the cooled chocolate milk. Add the cinnamon.

Pour the mixture into the top of a double boiler or a heavy saucepan. Simmer, stirring often with a wooden spoon, until the mixture thickens. Remove from the heat and stir in the vanilla. Cool. Stir in the heavy cream.

3. Pour the custard into an ice cream machine and follow the manufacturer's instructions.

4. To make the Hot Fudge Sauce, combine the sugar, cocoa, heavy cream, and corn syrup in a heavy saucepan. Bring the mixture to a boil over medium heat, stirring often. Continue cooking for about 1 minute.

5. Remove the sauce from the heat and stir in the butter and vanilla. Stir until smooth. Serve hot over cold ice cream.

6. To assemble a sundae, position one or two scoops of chocolate ice cream in a deep dessert dish or sundae bowl. Spoon about ¼ cup Hot Fudge Sauce, or to taste, over cold ice cream. Top with a generous dollop of whipped cream, a sprinkle of chopped nuts, and a cherry perched on top.

CHOCOLATE ICE CREAM SODA
(Makes 1 serving)

3 tablespoons Hot Fudge Sauce (see Index) or commercial fudge syrup
2 tablespoons half-and-half or milk
Chilled carbonated water
2 scoops Chocolate Ice Cream (see Index)

Use a tall glass. Mix the fudge sauce and half-and-half. Fill the glass about two-thirds full of carbonated water; stir to combine the ingredients. Add one scoop of ice cream. Perch the second scoop on the edge of the

glass, allowing guests to slide it into the glass themselves. Serve immediately.

EGG CREAM
(Makes 1 serving)

A New York soda fountain delight.

3 tablespoons Hot Fudge Sauce (see Index) or commercial fudge syrup
¼ cup half-and-half or heavy cream
Chilled carbonated water

1. Mix sauce and the half-and-half in a tall glass. Stir in enough chilled carbonated water almost to fill the glass.

2. Mix and serve immediately. The Egg Cream will be foamy on top.

Chocolate Cake with Stewed Fruit

MAKES 8-10 SERVINGS

For generations bakers have been souring milk by adding lemon juice or vinegar. We have discovered that you can sour milk with flavored vinegar and impart a delicate essence to the cake batter. Here we use raspberry vinegar.

1½ cups all-purpose flour
1¼ teaspoons baking powder
¼ teaspoon baking soda
¼ teaspoon salt
2 ounces unsweetened chocolate, chopped
6 tablespoons unsalted butter at room temperature
¾ cup granulated sugar
2 large eggs at room temperature
½ cup milk mixed with 1½ teaspoons raspberry vinegar
1 teaspoon vanilla extract
¾ cup stewed pitted prunes, pureed
½ cup golden raisins
Confectioners' sugar for sprinkling on cake

1. Set a rack in the center of the oven and preheat to 350°F. Grease and flour a 6-cup decorative ring mold, a 9″ × 5″ × 3″ loaf pan, or another 6-cup pan.

2. Sift the flour, baking powder, baking soda, and salt. Set aside.

3. Melt the chocolate in a small glass bowl in a

microwave for 2 minutes or in the top of a double boiler over but not touching simmering water. Stir until smooth. Cool.

4. In the large bowl of an electric mixer, cream the butter and sugar until light, about 1-2 minutes. Add the eggs, one at a time, beating well after each addition. Add the melted chocolate and beat until combined.

5. Add the sifted ingredients to the batter alternately with the sour milk. Stir in the vanilla. Stir the pureed prunes and raisins into the batter.

6. Pour the batter into the prepared pan and bake for 45-50 minutes or until a toothpick or bamboo skewer inserted in the center of the cake comes out clean and dry. Allow the cake to cool in the pan on a rack for 5 minutes. Invert the cake onto the wire rack to cool completely. Sprinkle with confectioners' sugar.

White Chocolate Pound Cake with Caramel Sauce

MAKES 8 SERVINGS

Serve thin slices of the Chocolate Pound Cake (see Index) and this White Chocolate Pound Cake together with Caramel Sauce. The White Chocolate Pound Cake can also be served plain or with fruit.

Note: To cream butter, cut it into ½-to ¾-inch pieces.

CAKE
2 cups all-purpose flour
¾ teaspoon baking powder
¼ teaspoon salt
3 ounces white chocolate, coarsely chopped
6 tablespoons unsalted butter at room temperature
1¼ cups granulated sugar
3 large eggs at room temperature
⅔ cup heavy cream
1 teaspoon vanilla extract

CARAMEL SAUCE
(Makes about 1½ cups)

¾ cup evaporated milk
1 cup lightly packed light brown sugar
½ cup granulated sugar
4 tablespoons (½ stick) unsalted butter
2 tablespoons light corn syrup
1 teaspoon vanilla extract

1. Set a rack in the center of the oven and preheat to 350°F. Grease and flour a 9″ × 5″ × 3″ loaf pan.

2. Sift the flour, baking powder, and salt together. Set aside.

3. Melt the white chocolate in a small glass bowl in the microwave or in the top of a double boiler over but not touching simmering water. Stir until smooth. Cool.

4. In the bowl of an electric mixer, cream the butter until light. Add the sugar and continue beating for 1-2 minutes. With a rubber spatula, scrape down the sides of the bowl. Add the eggs, one at a time, beating well after each addition. Blend in the cooled chocolate.

5. Add the flour mixture alternately with the cream. Add the vanilla and beat well.

6. Pour the batter into the prepared pan. Position pan in the center of the rack. Bake for 55 minutes or until a toothpick inserted into the cake comes out clean. Cool the cake in the pan on a rack for 5 minutes. To loosen the cake, run a knife around the inside edge of the pan. Invert the cake onto the wire rack and carefully invert it right side up. Cool the cake completely. To store the cake, cover it with aluminum foil and refrigerate.

7. For the sauce, in a heavy saucepan, combine the milk, sugars, butter, and corn syrup. Bring the mixture to a boil and reduce the heat to simmer. Continue cooking for about 3-4 minutes, whisking often. The sauce will thicken slightly. Remove it from the heat and stir in the vanilla. Cool.

8. Pour the sauce into a bowl, cover, and store in the refrigerator. The sauce is good hot or cold. To reheat, pour it into a saucepan and simmer until warm. Set a thin slice of cake or both chocolate and white cake slices on a plate. Spoon warm sauce around the cake.

Queen of Sheba Cake

MAKES 8 SERVINGS

The jewels in the crown of the Queen of Sheba Cake are the glistening blackberries and raspberries scattered in the vanilla sauce that surrounds the cake. Originating in France as a tribute to the famous queen, this is a moist, rich nut cake with subtle raspberry liqueur flavoring. Its history is shrouded in conflicting stories, but it seems that this adventurous beauty traveled a long distance from Arabia, carrying spices, fruits, jewels, and other riches, to talk about a trade route with King Solomon. We hope that she would be pleased with our modern-day tribute to her. We find that for best results it is necessary to use a springform pan.

CAKE

3 ounces semisweet chocolate, coarsely chopped

1 ounce unsweetened chocolate, coarsely chopped

4 large egg whites at room temperature

¾ cup sugar

½ teaspoon cream of tartar

½ cup cake flour

½ teaspoon baking powder

½ cup (1 stick) unsalted butter at room temperature

3 large egg yolks at room temperature

2 tablespoons raspberry liqueur

1 cup shelled almonds, ground fine

VANILLA SAUCE

2 cups heavy cream or half-and-half
4 large egg yolks at room temperature
¼ cup sugar
1½ teaspoons vanilla extract
½ cup heavy cream, chilled and whipped
1 cup fresh raspberries, washed and drained on paper towels
1 cup fresh blackberries, washed and drained on paper towels
16 blanched almonds

1. Set a rack in the center of the oven and preheat to 350°F. Butter and flour an 8-inch springform pan.

2. Melt the chocolates in a small glass bowl in a microwave or in the top of a double boiler over but not touching simmering water. When the chocolates are melted, stir to blend. Cool.

3. In the large bowl of an electric mixer, beat the egg whites until soft peaks form. Gently sprinkle with ¼ cup of the sugar and the cream of tartar. Continue beating until the egg whites are stiff but not dry. Set aside.

4. Sift the flour and baking powder together and set aside.

5. In the large bowl of an electric mixer, beat the butter with the remaining ½ cup sugar until light. Add the egg yolks, beating well after each addition. Blend in the cooled chocolate and the raspberry liqueur. Add the flour mixture and beat well. Sprinkle the almonds over the batter and incorporate.

6. Remove the bowl from the mixer and use a rubber

spatula to fold in about one-quarter of the beaten egg whites to lighten the batter. Fold in the remaining whites.

7. Using a rubber spatula, scrape the batter evenly into the prepared pan. Bake for about 30–35 minutes or until the cake just begins to shrink from the sides of the pan and a bamboo skewer or toothpick inserted in the center comes out almost dry (like a brownie) and comes out dry when inserted around the edges of the cake. Cool the cake on a wire rack. Run a small sharp knife around the inside edge of the pan and gently remove the rim. Leave the cake on the bottom of the pan to cool. Cover the cake with aluminum foil and refrigerate. It is best served at room temperature.

8. While the cake is cooling, prepare the sauce. Scald the cream in a small heavy saucepan. Cool.

9. In the small bowl of an electric mixer, beat the egg yolks with the sugar until light. Gradually, in a slow, steady stream, pour in the scalded cream, beating constantly. Spoon the mixture into the top of a double boiler and cook over but not touching simmering water until thickened, stirring often. Remove the sauce from the heat and spoon it into a bowl. Cool. Mix in the vanilla and stiffly beaten heavy cream.

10. To serve the cake, cut a slice and set it on a dessert dish. Spoon or ladle sauce around the cake. Scatter berries and nuts decoratively over the sauce and serve.

Hot Chocolate

MAKES 4 SERVINGS

"When you have breakfasted well and copiously, if you swallow a generous cup of good chocolate at the end of the meal, you will have digested everything perfectly three hours later."

From *The Physiology of Taste*, by Jean-Anthelme Brillat-Savarin, 1825

The most famous hot chocolate in Europe is served at Angelina's Tea Room, 226, rue de Rivoli, located across from the Tuileries in Paris. The service is purposely terrible so that visitors can sit and talk for hours without being disturbed. If you complain about the service, the waitress will ask you, in halting English, if you're American.

But the hot chocolate is so delicious that even if you're impatient the wait is worth it. Angelina's uses cream and real chocolate. And no one asks for a marshmallow.

We've worked out a healthier compromise using real milk chocolate and milk. Our recipe is less rich than that served at Angelina's, but it's delicious nonetheless. It's also easy to make. If desired, serve our Chocolate Kourambiethes (see Index) as an accompaniment.

4–6 ounces finest milk chocolate (1 to 1½ ounces per person, to taste)
3 cups whole milk
Whipped cream for garnish (optional)

1. Melt the chocolate in a small glass bowl in a microwave or in the top of a double boiler over but not touching simmering water. In a saucepan, heat milk *almost* to boiling, but don't let it boil, or a skin will form on the surface. Pour a little hot milk into the melted chocolate and mix well with a wire whisk. Add more milk and whisk again. Stir in the remaining milk and whisk until well mixed. Divide the chocolate among four mugs. Top with whipped cream if desired. Serve immediately.

Alternate Method: Put 1 to 1½ ounces milk chocolate in the bottom of each of four mugs. Microwave the mugs in 30-second increments until the chocolate is melted. Proceed as directed, dividing the milk among the mugs.

Note: If you substitute semisweet, bittersweet, or dark sweet chocolate for the milk chocolate in this recipe, you may need to add sugar to taste.

Chocolate Cupcakes with Chocolate Buttercream Frosting

MAKES 18 CUPCAKES

We have rediscovered the charm of the cupcake. Once it was a household specialty, and now it has all but disappeared from the modern cookbook. Our cupcake is light and spongy with a rich buttercream frosting.

CUPCAKES
2 cups all-purpose flour
1¼ teaspoons baking soda
¼ teaspoon salt
½ cup (1 stick) unsalted butter at room temperature
1½ cups granulated sugar
2 large eggs
3 ounces unsweetened chocolate, chopped, melted, and cooled
1¼ cups buttermilk
1 teaspoon vanilla extract

CHOCOLATE BUTTERCREAM FROSTING
10 tablespoons unsalted butter at room temperature
1 pound confectioners' sugar, sifted
2 ounces bittersweet chocolate, chopped, melted, and cooled
⅛ teaspoon salt
¼ cup half-and-half, cream, or buttermilk
1 teaspoon vanilla extract

1. Set a rack in the center of the oven and preheat to 350°F. Arrange 18 paper liners in cupcake pans.

2. Sift together the flour, baking soda, and salt. Set aside.

3. In the large bowl of an electric mixer, cream the butter and sugar together until light. Add the eggs, one at a time, beating well after each addition. Blend in the cooled chocolate. Add the flour mixture alternately with the buttermilk. Blend in the vanilla.

4. Fill the cupcake liners two-thirds full of batter. Bake for 20–25 minutes or until a toothpick or bamboo skewer inserted in the center of a cupcake comes out clean. Cool the cupcakes on a rack for 3–4 minutes before removing them from the pans. Cool completely on a wire rack.

5. While the cupcakes are cooling, prepare the frosting. In the large bowl of an electric mixer, cream the butter until light. Beat in the sugar, ½ cup at a time. Mix in the chocolate, salt, and enough half-and-half to produce the desired thickness. Stir in the vanilla. If the frosting is still too thick, add half-and-half by the teaspoon.

6. Spoon the frosting onto individual cupcakes and swirl over the top in a circular motion. Let the frosting set before serving. Chocolate Cupcakes should be served with a tall glass of chilled milk.

Note: We find that preparing the frosting in a food processor fitted with the steel blade makes it unnecessary to sift the sugar, so use a processor if preferred.

Chocolate Rum Soufflé

MAKES 8 SERVINGS

Part of the soufflé (steps 2, 3, and 4) can be prepared ahead of time, but you do have to excuse yourself from your guests and finish the soufflé at the last minute. It is well worth this trouble. The soufflé is a light yet satisfying, melt-in-your-mouth chocolate cloud with a slight rum overtone, baked and rushed to the table in all its glory. An airy, aromatic, fragile, and most elegant dessert, served at once before it deflates. The guests wait.

SOUFFLE
3 ounces semisweet chocolate, chopped
1 tablespoon unsalted butter
4 large egg yolks
⅓ cup sugar
2 tablespoons all-purpose flour
½ cup milk, scalded and cooled
3 tablespoons dark rum or dry sherry
6 large egg whites at room temperature
¼ teaspoon cream of tartar
¼ cup sugar

CHOCOLATE WHIPPED CREAM
1 cup heavy cream
3 tablespoons Dutch cocoa
¼ cup sugar
1 teaspoon vanilla extract

1. Set a rack in the lower third of the oven and preheat to 400°F. Butter and sugar a 6-cup soufflé dish.

Make a collar around the dish by wrapping a band of buttered and sugared aluminum foil around the dish about 1½-2½ inches above the rim. Attach the foil with tape. Set aside.

2. Melt the chocolate with the butter in a microwave or in the top of a double boiler over but not touching simmering water or in a heavy saucepan. Stir to combine the ingredients. Let cool.

3. Cook the egg yolks in a heavy saucepan over low heat for about 2 minutes, whisking almost constantly. Beat in ⅓ cup of sugar and continue beating until the sugar is dissolved and the mixture is light, another 2-3 minutes. Whisk in the flour and continue cooking until the flour is absorbed, about 1 minute.

4. Mix in the milk, the cooled chocolate mixture, and the rum.

5. Beat the egg whites in the large bowl of an electric mixer or by hand until soft peaks form. Sprinkle the cream of tartar and ¼ cup sugar over the egg whites and continue beating until stiff but not dry. Using a rubber spatula, fold about 1½ cups of the egg whites into the chocolate mixture to lighten it. Fold in the remaining whites.

6. Using a rubber spatula, spoon the batter into the prepared soufflé dish.

7. Reduce the heat to 375°F. Bake for 25-30 minutes or until the soufflé is puffed and set, to the touch, in the center.

8. Prepare the Chocolate Whipped Cream while the soufflé is baking. Beat the cream in an electric mixer or by hand until soft peaks form. Sift the cocoa over the cream and incorporate. Sprinkle the sugar over the

cream and incorporate. Continue beating until stiff peaks form; be careful not to overbeat. Stir in the vanilla.

9. Have the whipped cream at the table before removing the soufflé from the oven. Gently remove the collar from the soufflé. Rush the soufflé into the dining room. Spoon out the soufflé around the edges of the dish first and serve the center last. Using two tablespoons, spoon out soufflé onto each dessert dish and serve at once with a dollop of whipped cream.

Marbled Brownies

MAKES ONE 9-INCH SQUARE PAN
OR 16 BROWNIES

We've added cream cheese and chopped pecans to this classic cakelike brownie from the fifties. If you wish to omit the cheese, simply stir the pecans into the batter.

FILLING
9 ounces cream cheese at room temperature
½ cup granulated sugar
1 large egg
1 teaspoon vanilla extract
½ cup chopped pecans

BROWNIE LAYER
⅔ cup unsalted butter at room temperature
1½ cups lightly packed dark brown sugar
2 large eggs
1 teaspoon vanilla extract
¼ pound unsweetened chocolate, melted and cooled
½ teaspoon baking powder
⅔ cup all-purpose flour
Confectioners' sugar (optional)

1. Set a rack in the center of the oven and preheat to 350°F. Grease and flour a 9-inch square pan. For the filling, beat the cream cheese until soft. Add the sugar and beat until well combined, about 1 minute. Add the egg and vanilla and beat until mixed. Stir in the pecans.

2. Make the brownie layer in a separate bowl. Beat

the butter and brown sugar until combined. Beat in the eggs and vanilla. Add the chocolate and continue beating. Add the baking powder and flour and beat until well mixed, about 1 minute.

3. Spoon a *scant* half of the batter into the prepared pan. Bake for 10 minutes. Spoon the cream cheese filling over the partly baked layer. Spoon the remaining chocolate batter over the cheese filling. Swirl a spatula through the mixture to get a marbled effect.

4. Bake for 40 minutes or until a toothpick inserted in the center comes out almost dry. Remove from the oven and cool in the pan for 20 minutes on a wire rack. Carefully cut the brownies into bars with a sharp knife. Cool. Transfer the brownies to a serving platter and sift confectioners' sugar over the tops if desired.

Chocolate Pound Cake with Coffee Chocolate Sauce

MAKES 12 SERVINGS, ABOUT 1½ CUPS SAUCE

Pound cake was so named because it was originally made up of a pound each of flour, eggs, sugar, and butter. It is densely textured and can be sliced to any width, from cake slice to paper-thin servings. You can serve pound cake simply sprinkled with confectioners' sugar or enjoy it with a chocolate sauce.

CAKE
1¾ cups cake flour
⅓ cup unsweetened cocoa
½ teaspoon salt
½ teaspoon baking powder
10 tablespoons unsalted butter at room temperature
1¼ cups sugar
3 large eggs
1 tablespoon coffee liqueur
1 teaspoon vanilla extract
¾ cup sour cream

COFFEE CHOCOLATE SAUCE
2 ounces unsweetened chocolate, chopped
2 tablespoons unsalted butter
½ cup sugar
¾ cup evaporated milk
¼ cup coffee liqueur
½ teaspoon vanilla extract

1. Set a rack in the center of the oven and preheat to 350°F. Grease a 9″ × 5″ × 3″ loaf pan. Line the bottom of the pan with greased wax paper. Sift the flour, cocoa, salt, and baking powder together. Set aside.

2. In the large bowl of an electric mixer, cream the butter until light, about 1 minute. Add the sugar and continue beating for about 2 minutes. Add the eggs, one at a time; beat well after each addition. Mix in the coffee liqueur and vanilla.

3. Add the flour mixture alternately with the sour cream. Blend well after each addition.

4. Pour the batter into the prepared pan. Bake for 1 hour and 10 minutes or until a sharp knife or toothpick inserted in the center comes out clean. Cool the cake on a rack for 5 minutes. Loosen the cake by running a knife around the inside edges of the pan. Invert the cake onto a wire rack and then carefully invert it right side up. Cool the cake completely.

5. While the cake is cooling, prepare the sauce. First melt the chocolate and butter in the top of a double boiler over but not touching simmering water or in a small glass dish in the microwave. Stir until the chocolate is smooth. Cool.

6. Using a spatula, scrape the chocolate mixture into a bowl. Mix in the sugar, milk, liqueur, and vanilla.

7. Cover the sauce with plastic wrap and store in the refrigerator until serving time. The sauce can be served cold or warm.

8. Set a slice of cake in a pool of the sauce to serve. To store the cake, cover it with aluminum foil or plastic wrap and store at room temperature or in the refrigerator. Pound cake keeps well for up to 2 weeks.

English Toffee

MAKES ABOUT 1 POUND

For the perfect English Toffee, each piece should be dipped individually in the chocolate and then rolled in the nuts. This provides maximum chocolate coverage. Here, however, we do it the traditional and less laborious way.

¾ cup finely chopped pecans or walnuts
Candy thermometer
1 cup (2 sticks) unsalted butter
1 cup sugar
2 tablespoons water
1 tablespoon light corn syrup
¼ pound semisweet chocolate, chopped, melted and cooled

1. Butter a 13″ × 9″ pan. Sprinkle half the nuts over the bottom of the pan.

2. In a medium-size heavy saucepan fitted with a candy thermometer, melt the butter over low heat. Whisk in the sugar; cook over low heat, stirring constantly, until the mixture comes to a rolling boil.

3. Stir in the water and corn syrup, mixing well. Continue cooking, stirring often, until the mixture reaches 290°F.

4. Pour the candy into the prepared pan, spreading it evenly with the back of a spoon. When the toffee has cooled, spread the melted chocolate evenly over the toffee, again using the back of a spoon. Sprinkle the toffee with

the remaining nuts. Refrigerate until set. (I bought a large marble tile that is reserved for toffee making. The cool surface of the marble cools the toffee quickly.)

5. When the toffee is hard, break it into irregular serving-size pieces. Set in a candy dish and serve. Store toffee in a covered container.

Brownstone Front Cake

MAKES ONE 9″ × 13″ UNFROSTED CAKE
OR 12 SERVINGS

Named after New York's brownstones, our very chocolaty, easy-to-make cake in a glass dish was popular in the forties and remains so among a small group of devotees. It is absolutely delicious. The butter gives it good keeping qualities. Serve it unfrosted, with a decorative sprinkling of confectioners' sugar. If there's any left, leave it in the glass dish. Store it tightly covered with plastic wrap or place it in a plastic bag with a twister seal.

1½ cups (3 sticks) unsalted butter at room temperature
1¾ cups lightly packed dark brown sugar
4 large eggs, separated, at room temperature
¼ pound unsweetened chocolate, melted
2 teaspoons vanilla extract
2½ teaspoons baking powder
Scant 3 cups sifted cake flour
1 cup plus 1 tablespoon milk
⅛ teaspoon cream of tartar
¼ cup granulated sugar
1 large lacy-patterned doily
Confectioners' sugar

1. Set a rack in the center of the oven and preheat to 350°F. Liberally grease and flour a 9″ × 13″ glass baking dish.

2. In the large bowl of an electric mixer, beat the butter until soft. Add the brown sugar and beat until

well mixed. Add the egg yolks, one at a time, beating well after each addition, about 1 minute. Add the melted chocolate and vanilla and beat again.

3. Add the baking powder and sifted cake flour alternately with the milk, beginning and ending with flour.

4. Beat the egg whites until they hold soft peaks. Add the cream of tartar. Continue beating until stiff. With the beaters running, pour the granulated sugar into the egg whites in a steady stream and beat until the meringue is stiff.

5. Spoon the batter over the meringue and fold together lightly but thoroughly until no unmixed patches remain. Spoon the batter into the prepared baking dish.

6. Bake for 50 minutes or until a toothpick inserted in the center comes out clean and dry. Let the cake sit in the dish on a wire rack for 5 minutes. Invert the cake onto a large plate, then invert it onto a cooling rack, top side up, to avoid marks on top of the cake. Wash the glass baking dish.

7. When cool, return the cake to the clean dish. Place a doily over the cake. Sprinkle confectioners' sugar liberally over the doily. Lift carefully. There will be a lacy pattern on top of the cake. Cut into squares to serve.

Great American Chocolate Cake

MAKES THREE 10-INCH LAYERS
OR 12-16 SERVINGS

This is such a splendid cake that we've made it in three 10-inch layers. The cake is filled and frosted with a cooked chocolate fudge frosting. Borrowing an idea from the Viennese Sacher Torte, we've added a layer of strained raspberry jam under the frosting.

CAKE
6 ounces unsweetened chocolate, coarsely chopped
1 cup boiling water
1⅓ cups unsalted butter at room temperature
3 cups lightly packed dark brown sugar
6 large eggs
2 teaspoons vanilla extract
4 teaspoons baking powder
1 teaspoon baking soda
4 cups sifted cake flour
2 cups buttermilk

UNDERCOATING
1–1¼ cups strained raspberry jam

CHOCOLATE FUDGE FROSTING
4 cups lightly packed light or dark brown sugar
¼ cup light or dark corn syrup
1⅓ cups milk
Candy thermometer

4½ ounces unsweetened chocolate, coarsely chopped
½ cup (1 stick) unsalted butter, cut into chunks
2 teaspoons vanilla extract

1. Set a rack in the center of the oven and preheat to 350°F. Generously grease three 10-inch round cake pans. Line the bottom with wax paper or parchment cut to fit and grease the paper. Place the chocolate in a small bowl and cover with boiling water. In the large bowl of an electric mixer, beat the butter until soft. Add the brown sugar and beat until well mixed. Add the eggs, one at a time, beating after each addition, about 1 minute.

2. Add the chocolate/water mixture and vanilla and beat until well combined. Beat in the baking powder and baking soda. Add the flour alternately with the buttermilk, beginning and ending with the flour.

3. Divide the batter evenly among the prepared pans. Bake for 30–35 minutes or until a toothpick inserted in the center comes out clean and dry. Let sit in the pans for 5 minutes on a wire rack. Turn the layers out onto the wire rack to cool. Carefully peel off the wax paper.

4. For the filling, press the raspberry jam through a strainer with a wooden spoon. Discard the seeds. When the layers cool, cover the top and sides of each with jam. Do not stack the layers. Refrigerate them to set the jam while you make the frosting.

5. For the frosting, place the brown sugar, corn syrup, and milk in a large heavy-bottomed saucepan and stir to combine. Set a candy thermometer in place and cook without stirring until the thermometer registers 234°F.

6. Immediately remove the pan from the heat and add the chocolate, mixing well with a wooden spoon.

Add the butter without stirring. It will melt on top of the chocolate and form a protective layer. Let sit for 1 hour without mixing or disturbing in any way.

7. After 1 hour, transfer the frosting to the bowl of an electric mixer and add the vanilla. Beat for several minutes, until thick and spreadable. If the frosting becomes too thick, beat in hot water, 1 teaspoon at a time, until creamy enough to spread.

8. Cover the edges of a serving plate with wax paper strips. Place one raspberry-covered layer on the wax paper. Frost the layer with chocolate frosting. Arrange a second layer on the first. Frost the layer with chocolate frosting. Arrange a third layer on top. Frost the sides with chocolate frosting, then frost the top of the cake. Allow the frosting to set. Gently remove the strips of wax paper.

Meringue Cake

MAKES TWO 9-INCH LAYERS OR 8 SERVINGS

The meringue is baked along with the batter in this unusual cake that was popular in the East in the forties and fifties. One layer is then placed meringue side down and topped with a whipped cream filling. The second layer is then arranged on the filling, meringue side up. Our chocolate version is equally beautiful and even more delicious than the original.

Note: Do not substitute semisweet chocolate morsels for the milk chocolate because the cake will taste too bitter. Also, since this cake must be baked in nonstick pans, and some have a tendency to brown layers too quickly, we suggest an insulating technique: either place the cake pans on an insulated cookie sheet during baking or invert a cookie sheet with raised sides, place it on the oven rack, and bake the layers on it.

CAKE

½ cup (1 stick) unsalted butter at room temperature
½ cup lightly packed dark brown sugar
4 large egg yolks
¼ cup half-and-half
1 teaspoon vanilla extract
14 tablespoons sifted cake flour
2 tablespoons unsweetened cocoa, sifted
1 teaspoon baking powder
¼–⅓ cup milk chocolate morsels

MERINGUE
4 large egg whites at room temperature
⅛ teaspoon cream of tartar
1 cup granulated sugar
1 teaspoon vanilla extract

WHIPPED CREAM FILLING
¾ cup heavy cream
2 tablespoons confectioners' sugar

1. Set a rack in the center of the oven and preheat to 325°F. Liberally grease and flour two 9-inch *nonstick* round cake pans. For the cake, in the large bowl of an electric mixer, beat the butter and brown sugar until well combined. Add the egg yolks and beat again; then add the half-and-half and vanilla and beat again. Beat in the cake flour, cocoa, and baking powder. Stir in the chocolate morsels. Use a spatula to spread the batter in the prepared pans.

2. For the meringue, beat the egg whites until they hold soft peaks. Add the cream of tartar and beat until stiff. Add the granulated sugar in a thin stream; add the vanilla quickly and turn off the beaters as soon as it is mixed in. Spread the meringue over the layers. Be sure the meringue touches the pan sides at all points around the rims.

3. Invert a cookie sheet with raised sides and place it on the oven rack. Set the cake pans on the cookie sheet and bake for 30 minutes. The meringue will be lightly browned.

4. The layers must cool in the pans. When cool, invert one layer (the least attractive one) meringue side down onto a serving platter.

5. For the filling, whip the cream until stiff. Mix in the confectioners' sugar. Spread over the bottom layer. Top with the second layer, meringue side up. Cover the cake lightly and refrigerate until ready to serve.

Truffles

MAKES 30 SMALL TRUFFLES

These small, irregularly shaped French-style truffles resemble real truffles more than the large, uniformly round candies found in American candy stores. And they're easy to make. Serve them with fresh fruit such as whole strawberries, peeled pineapple chunks, or unpeeled pear wedges sprinkled with raspberries.

French-style truffles are usually rolled in unsweetened cocoa. If you like a sweeter coating, roll them in a mixture of 2 tablespoons each confectioners' sugar and cocoa.

1 ounce (about 2 tablespoons plus 1 teaspoon) mint chocolate morsels
3 ounces semisweet chocolate
3½ tablespoons unsalted butter
1 large egg yolk
3 tablespoons milk
¼ cup unsweetened cocoa

1. Melt the mint morsels, semisweet chocolate, and butter together in a glass bowl in a microwave or in the top of a double boiler over but not touching simmering water. Stir in the egg yolk and milk, mixing well. Transfer to a bowl and cover. Refrigerate for 40 minutes or until the mixture holds its shape.

2. Sift the cocoa through a strainer onto a flat plate. Form the chocolate mixture into small, irregularly shaped ovals the size of a Brazil nut. Roll into the cocoa and place on a serving platter. When all the truffles are made, sift the remaining cocoa over the platter.

Chocolate Angel Pie

MAKES ONE 9-INCH PIE OR 6–8 SERVINGS

Here's a delicious classic from the forties and fifties.

ITALIAN MERINGUE CRUST
¾ cup sugar
6 tablespoons water
Candy thermometer
3 large egg whites at room temperature
1½ cups chopped pecans

CHOCOLATE CREAM FILLING
*3 ounces dark sweet eating-quality chocolate (*not *semisweet or bittersweet)*
1½ cups heavy cream
A piece of dark sweet chocolate for decorative shavings

1. Set a rack in the center of the oven and preheat to 275°F. Butter a 9-inch pie pan. Place the sugar and water in a heavy-bottomed saucepan fitted with a candy thermometer and heat to 234°F. Meanwhile, beat the egg whites until stiff. With the beaters running, pour the hot syrup over the egg whites in a thin stream. Continue beating until the meringue is thick.

2. Fold the pecans into the meringue. Spoon it into the prepared pie pan to cover the bottom and sides. Bake for 50–60 minutes or until the meringue has dried and is golden brown. Let cool at room temperature.

3. For the filling, melt the chocolate in a small glass bowl in a microwave or in the top of a double boiler over

but not touching simmering water. Allow it to cool slightly. Whip the cream until stiff. Remove 1 cup of the whipped cream and reserve to spread on top of the pie. Fold the chocolate into the remaining whipped cream. Spoon the chocolate into the cooled meringue shell.

4. Carefully spread the reserved whipped cream over the top. Using a vegetable peeler, shave a piece of chocolate over the pie so the shavings decorate the top.

Sources

Chocolate for baking can be mail-ordered from the following sources.

Albert Uster Imports, Inc.
9211 Gaither Rd.
Gaithersburg, MD 20877
1-800-231-8154

•

Dairy Fresh Chocolate
57 Salem St.
Boston, MA 02113
1-800-336-5536

•

Gourmail
126 Pleasant Valley St.
No. 401
Methuen, MA 01844
1-800-366-5900

•

Istanbul Express
2434 Durant Ave
Berkeley, CA 94704

•

Maid of Scandinavia
3244 Raleigh Ave.
Minneapolis, MN 55415
1-800-328-6722

•

Paprika Weiss Importer
1572 Second Ave
New York, NY 10028

•

The Sweet Shop
P.O. Box 573
Ft. Worth, TX 76101
1-800-222-2269

•

World's Finest Chocolate, Inc.
4801 S. Lawndale Ave.
Chicago, IL 60632-3062

Index